PRESENT *in the* PAST

A Collection of American Historical Documents,
Volume Two

Edited by
Brian Hart
Del Mar College

Kendall Hunt
publishing company

ISBN 978-0-7575-6306-5

Printed in the United States of America
10 9 8 7 6 5 4 3

CONTENTS

SECTION 3

Documents of War: The United States, World War II, and the Early Cold War, 1940s–1950s **55**

SECTION 4

The Struggle for Equality and the Longest War, 1950s–1960s **77**

SECTION 5

SECTION 1

AMERICA AND AMERICANS AFTER THE CIVIL WAR, 1865–1900

1 Northerners and Southerners Ponder the Future, 1865

STAUNTON SPECTATOR, "LO! THE POOR NEGRO," APRIL 10, 1866

The Spectator *argues that "the emancipation of the negro heralds the doom of his race," and believes that the colonization of American blacks in another country represents their best chance for survival. The idea of colonizing free blacks in a remote country or on the western frontier had been discussed for decades before the Civil War, as most whites in the United States could not conceive of African Americans living among them in equality.*

What is to become of the negro? This is a question which now addresses itself to the minds of all reflecting men. Shall he remain here where he will be brought into ruinous competition with a superior race, or shall he seek a home elsewhere? If he remain here, poverty, wretchedness, and ultimate extinction will be his sad fate. If it were not that we have the kindest feelings for the negroes, we should like to see them move into the Northern States, that they might test the friendship of the Northern people for them. We are satisfied that the best friends of the negroes are the people of the South, who, with few exceptions, have for them none other than kind feelings. The Southern people do not blame the negroes for anything which has occurred. Their emancipation, which we believe to be a curse instead of a blessing to them, was effected without any agency of theirs. They, as a mass, acted well and faithfully during the war, and have comported themselves remarkably well since the war. No blame attaches to them, and this the Southern people appreciate and acknowledge, and hence attach no culpability to the negro.

If the negroes are to be considered the *wards* of the Government, and this guardianship is to continue for an indefinite time, we think that they should be distributed among the several States of the Union, North and South, in proportion to the population of the several States. In this way, the *blessing* would be equitably distributed, and none could complain that they were denied their just share of it.

But as we know, notwithstanding their loud professions of friendship, that the people of the Northern States do not desire, the negroes to become residents of their States, would treat them worse than the Southern people ever did, or ever will do, we must decide whether it is better for them to remain in the Southern States, in unequal and ruinous competition with the whites, or to seek a home in some favorite clime where they can live to themselves and for themselves alone. If the latter could be, it should be done. We confess that we fear the emancipation of the negro heralds the doom of his race. Are they willing to be colonized, and can colonization be rendered practicable? We will recur to this subject in future.

NELSON IRWIN TO JOHN M. SCHOFIELD, OCTOBER 8, 1866

Nelson Irwin, an African American in Augusta County, writes to General John Schofield, the military commander of Virginia, pleading for protection and justice on behalf of the freedmen. Citing the recent imprisonment of several black men in Staunton, Nelson argues that freedom for blacks under such circumstances remained "meaningless tyranny." For ex-slaves in Augusta, as in most parts of the South, the Freedmen's Bureau was usually the only government agency they could appeal to for protection—and even the Bureau could not prevent much of the violence that freedmen endured during the postwar era.

Staunton
Oct. 8th 1866

General

Living within your military department, I am forced to appeal to you in my own behalf. My case and cause are those of thousands and just as I am effected they will be effected also. There is a deep laid organization here that governs and controls every thing by might in defiance of truth and justice. On any, even the least pretense a black man is taken up and imprisoned. His color is his condemnation, and every lawless act committed he is accused of. At present my brethern are living in a reign of terror and many of them are locked up in Staunton Gaol Jail.

An act of theft has been committed here by one or two black men and lo! four are taken up and all of us are accused. Some of us had to fly, who were and are as innocent of the crime as you are. The Freedmen's bureau is ineffective, laughed at and despised. On the first Monday of November these men are to be tried, and in view of their case we cannot expect justice unless the strong arm of military protection is reached out to us. We gave to the rich white man our best years, our strength, our youth, our sweat, and now that we are free, we get in return meaness, tyranny and injustice.

And now General, instruct the officers of Bureau and let them insist on justice. Some of our men are in a state of perpetual terror. If you turn your back on us, who can we appeal to. If we have committed a violation of law let us be judged impartially by the laws, but let us not be condemned with out a cause. From this depth of degredation we look to you, and in the name of suffering humanity, I trust I do not write in vain.

The name of those imprisoned are Reuben Hill, James Burgy, Joe Wilson is out as State evidence, and mind you a black man's oath before the war would not be believed and now they would degrade him to be a liar. General we only ask for justice. See that we will have it and all will be yet well. There is no accusation against me and there never was. I am black but in my heart there is not stain of infamy.

I am General
Your very humble Srvt
Nelson Irwin

STATEMENT OF ISABELLA BURTON, JANUARY 17, 1868

Isabella Burton provides information to the Freedmen's Bureau office in Augusta about her two sons, who had been sold by her master before the end of the war, in hopes of finding her children. Ex-slaves across the South sought desperately to find loved ones who had been sold away from their families during slavery, and often appealed to the Bureau for assistance in their searches. Isabella still lived alone in 1870, when the census officials for Augusta came to her home, and there is no record that she ever found her children.

Isabella Burton (Mother)

Horace Bucker sold my two sons (seven & five years age) Benjamin & Horace, sold to Larke & Wright in Maddison County Va. Johnny Gilgarnett & Jeremiah Gilgarnett were playmates.

I am living in Staunton Now a widow & alone, would like very much to see them.

THOMAS P. JACKSON TO ORLANDO BROWN, MARCH 24, 1868

Thomas Jackson, agent for the Freedmen's Bureau in Augusta from April 1867 to March 1868, reports to the regional office in Richmond about the general condition of the county, the problems faced by the freedmen, the persistent antagonism between local blacks and whites, and current divisions within Augusta over the political future of Virginia. Field agents such as Jackson were required to file monthly reports detailing local conditions in their jurisdiction.

Brig Genl O. Brown
Asst Comr District of Va. Richmond (Through HdQrs 9th Sub Dist Va)
Staunton, Va.
March 24, 1868

General
In compliance with C.O. No. 6 S. 1866 B.R.F.&A.L. I have the honor to make the following report of condition of Bureau Affairs in 4 Div. 9 S. Dist Va. comprizing the counties of Augusta & Highland.

Settlements of wages for labor in 1867 are generally concluded, still this office is much sought by freedpeople asking aid and advice on the many questions of account which ever arise between employer and employed. With some exceptions, more than is desirable, but less than could be expected, considering their recent condition of ignorant servitude, freedmen in this Division are industrious and orderly. Surplus earnings of last year have been largely expended in bridging over the long winter, but save in cases of sickness or desertion there has not been much actual suffering. There is much diversity of employment in this Division—farming, coaling, in connection with iron mining, rail road repairs, and supplies of fuel, &c preparing material for building, such as brick, lumber &c and this causes more regular demand for labor than in a purely agricultural district. If freedmen could but better understand the value of time and short intelligent money reckonings, they would advance much more rapidly in material prosperity. The desire to own a homestead is general, but the plan pursued by many freedmen is fraught with great danger, if by any disaster present system kind officers should retain power. Purchases are made with agreement to make so many annual payments and when purchase money is all paid then a deed to be received. Unless where I can influence them, most take but a simple receipt and may have to sue for title, but I advise all to have a legal contract drawn executed and recorded, but many do not. Written contracts for labor by the year for 1868 are not so general as usual. As I have before reported I think the change to casual hire will in the end prove a disadvantage to the laborer and have advised permanent contracts through this office. The social and moral condition of freedmen is not what it should be. The vices engendered by slavery are too deeply rooted to be easily eradicated and I fear until the community at large realize that the freedman is a citizen and seek to elevate him by example and precept, he will in many respects disappoint his friends. The relations of freedmen and whites to each other is in an unsatisfactory condition. The pernicious teachings of the conservative leaders and press have unbounded effect on ignorant whites, who look upon the freedmen with contempt and hate and do not hesitate to use violence where their leaders use abusive language. Assaults on freedmen during this month have been trifling except attack on Jefferson Davison (c) by William Hite and Joseph Trimble. The wounds caused by a stone, the pistol though drawn not fired. This case is referred to Mr. Joseph Wilson J. P. for investigation. The political relations of white and colored to each other are directly antagonistic. The conservative leaders have through District Superintendents, Chiefs of 50 & Captains of 10 fully organized themselves to defeat the Constitution about to be submitted to the people of Va. I do not anticipate there will be any armed and organized public demonstration to drive voters to or from the polls but every effort short of what would necessitate military interference will be used to secure the defeat of the Constitution no matter what its provisions. No progress has been made by me in organizing Temperance Associations in this Division. I have striven earnestly to establish such societies but without any success. There is not much drunkeness among freedmen here but there is more spirits drank than is good for them even were their circumstances better than they are.

I have the honor to be, General
Your obt servt
Thos P Jackson
Asst Sub Asst Comr

JOHN W. JORDAN TO JOHN A. MCDONNELL, MAY 4, 1868

John Jordan, Freedmen's Bureau agent in Augusta from April to August 1868, reports to his commanding officer in Winchester on the appearance of the Ku Klux Klan in Staunton. The Klan emerged during the late 1860s as a loosely organized movement that served as a means for frustrated white Southerners to influence local political and social development through terror and intimidation.

Capt. Jno A. McDonnell
Sub Asst Comr
Winchester, Va

Staunton, Va.
May 4th 1868

Capt.

I have the honor to call your attention to certain demonstrations made by an organization here known as the "Ku Klux Klan" and which have caused a vast deal of dangerous excitement, especially among the colored population and which if not promptly suppressed will culminate in serious and deplorable disturbances of the public peace.

This Klan made their appearance in the Streets of Staunton about 1 o'clock Sunday morning last, mounted and the Klan being enmasked in white sheets or something of the kind, and being armed caused no little consternation among the colored people and much serious annoyance to the respectable whites. Their operations were attended with the discharge of pistols and also by cheers or yelling, which of course occurring as it did almost in the center of the town aroused almost the entire population.

On yesterday I addressed a formal communication to the Mayor upon the subject who has informed me that every effort is being made by the Civil Authorities to ferret out the guilty parties in the matter, who I am assured will be brought to punishment and the operations of the Klan suppressed at once.

The colored people are very much excited upon the subject and but little is needed to bring about a serious state of things here. I would also remark that I have reported the facts to the Military Comr for this Division also.

I am Capt
Your obt Svt
Jno W. Jordan
A.S.A. Comr &c
B. of R. F. & A. L.

2. FRANKLIN COUNTY

FRANKLIN REPOSITORY, "FREEDMEN," FEBRUARY 8, 1865

With the war nearly over, the Repository *considers what will become of blacks in the United States once the slaves of the South are all liberated. Arguing that blacks will make good citizens (as evinced by their distinguished service as soldiers, and their accomplishments as a race), the* Repository *argues that freedmen should be educated, provided moral instruction, and given economic opportunities. While many Republicans believed that the freedmen deserved support in the postwar era, others in the party were also motivated by the fact that the Republicans depended heavily upon black votes in the South to remain dominant in national elections.*

Since the skies of our national horizon are beginning to look bright, and the dark and threatening clouds of war disappearing, the question is often asked, what shall be done with the freedmen? We confess the question easier asked than answered, yet it may be never so difficult, it must be answered, and that too, in a way becoming a free intelligent and christian people. Whilst the war lasts, but one duty remains, that is, to keep up our armies to their full complement, and supply them with every thing necessary to prosecute the war vigorously and successfully. We have Generals the ablest and bravest in the world, and who have the full confidence of the people. The last election was but a warrant to them from the people to use all means necessary to suppress the rebellion, and conquer a lasting and permanent peace.

This they are doing as fast as the most sanguine could ask. Victory everywhere perches proudly upon our banners and as the southern traitors are yielding and our armies marching unmolested through their borders; the civil authorities are tacitly seeking terms of compromise and peace honorable to themselves if possible. Whilst the affairs in the field stand so favorable, we find nearly one million of freedmen, and the number daily increasing, accessible to the people of the loyal States. They are ignorant, stupid in many cases, and passive recipients of the first influences which strike them. The transition from slavery to freedmen has doubtless jostled their minds a little, and developed new hopes and desires, and prepared them to hear and think as they never could before. The proper instruction will elevate them rapidly—wrong influence will make them more miserable than they were before emancipation. If we do not carry them light, truth, strength and courage, they will inevitably sink under the flood tide of vices which follow an army. Their usefulness has been fairly tested, they have entered the ranks, have shown good capacity in acquiring knowledge sufficient to make good soldiers, and at Fort Wagner; in front of Petersburg and elsewhere, they have shown themselves equal to the best soldiers. No one who speaks dispassionately upon the subject will say that they will not make courageous and available soldiers. They have on more than one occasion received the commendation of their Generals for valuable and efficient services.

That they make good mechanics is fairly proven by the fact, that many of them are such, even in the degraded condition of Slavery. They are found in almost every one of the rougher trades, and skilled equal to any even of our own race, who labor in the same occupations. In many parts of the South, it was no unusual thing for planters, to have all the necessary mechanics among his slaves, and the slaves were valued according to their skill in whatever trade they were taught. They are proverbial for their powers of imitation. They are as a general thing fond of music and acquire it easily, and always where they have the least opportunity become excellent performers. We find even some without the advantages of instruction, or much opportunity for practice become quite proficient.

But we need not stop here, we find them entering the learned and honorable professions. We have them in the ministry, and doing much honor to the profession. We have them in the profession of medicine, editing newspapers, and but a few days since on motion of Hon. Charles Summer, one Brooks was admitted to practice law in the Supreme court of the United States. This man Brooks is admitted to be gifted with extraordinary intellectual powers, and although young in years, stands at the head of the profession he has chosen for himself.

What then shall be done with the freedmen? Shall we allow them to look out for themselves and provide for their wants as best they can? Shall we keep open our stables and employ them as hostlers, use them as waiters at our dining tables, servants anywhere and everywhere? Or shall we colonize them and send them to some other part of the globe, as an inferior and useless race. No, none of these. There is a higher duty required of us, and our own national salvation demands it. We must come to their help, and pour in upon them the inspiration of a higher and better life; they must be taught to read and write, under the tuition of religious teachers, and in this way, they will be elevated very rapidly and enjoy the blessings of liberty.

We are bound by many considerations to come to their help. They are a part of our fallen race, and from this part, we are required by the spirit and aim of the religion we profess to save all the lost that is possible. They have been degraded and oppressed by our nation, and we have for years denounced the institution that bound them to the earth. We therefore owe them more than common benevolence to amend for the injury we have done them. If we therefore at once fit them for the position of freemen; if they are made intelligent, virtuous, industrious, they will prove a great blessing to themselves and the nation, but if they are left in ignorance, the victims of loose and vile men, they will prove a curse to themselves and our country.

In many parts of the country societies are organized for the purpose of raising funds to send teachers among them. This is a step in the right direction. Let the right kind of teachers among them. This is a step in the right direction. Let the right kind of teachers be sent, and plenty of them, and it will not be long until a new era shall dawn upon our country, and we can truthfully say, that our country is, "the land of the free" "and the home of the brave." If history be true, our own race were as degraded intellectually when the Romans invaded Britain, as ever the African race was, yet by moral and intellectual training, it has surpassed all others, and now stands the most powerful and enlightened race upon the face of the earth.

What may be done with the African race in the future we cannot tell. We know they have capacity, and this being the land of their birth, our duty is with the present. That they have giants among them even in their degraded condition does not admit of a doubt. In this broad land of ours, under the blessing of our Government, they can be made useful to themselves, the country and posterity. Let it the effort be fairly made.

2 Conditions in the South, 1865–1867

WILLIAM GILMORE SIMMS

As the Civil War ended, Southerners began to consider the losses suffered in the four-year conflict. Few lost as much as or sank more quickly into poverty than William Gilmore Simms, one of the most important writers in the antebellum South. The son of a poor immigrant tradesman, Simms had risen rapidly to a position of affluence and leadership. Thus, during the war he was a strong supporter of slavery and the Confederacy. However, the war destroyed his society and with it his place in society; he was near destitution with nine persons to support on a mere $10 per week. Most of his letters in these years dealt with his impoverished condition. Writing from Columbia, South Carolina, to a friend in the North, Simms poured out his sad story and asked for help.

Columbia, S. C.
June 13, 1865.

My dear Lawson.

I have a chance of writing you, but only a few moments. I have written you repeatedly, by parties going north, mostly returning soldiers, but half doubt whether you have received any of my letters. If you have not you have yet to learn that my house, newly rebuilt, has been destroyed by Sherman's army; my stables, carriage house, barns, gin house, machine and threshing houses; in short every building of any value; my mules, horses, cattle driven off & carried away, or butchered; my wagons, ploughs, implements, all destroyed; and I am here, temporarily destitute, without money to spare to telegraph you. I am sleeping in a garret, so are my daughters, Mary L. & Chevillette. Augusta, with her own daughter, & my two little boys are living with Mrs. Rivers at the little village of Bamberg, with barely bread enough to support life. I earn here a small pittance weekly, by editing a paper, newly started in this place, which does not yet pay. Two weeks ago, I was summoned by telegraph to my son, Gilmore, who lay dangerously ill, in the town of Chester, some 65 miles off. He had typhoid fever. I had to borrow the money, a trifle, to eke out the little I had, in order to get to him—had to travel in a wagon, all the railways being destroyed. I found him delirious, raving, & without sleep for 5 days. By the blessings of the Good God he is spared; and the crisis terminated favorably. I left him convalescent & out of all danger, but too feeble to travel, and had to leave him, to see to my duties here & my other children. Thirty of my negroes were carried off by Sherman's Army; the rest are at work, after a fashion, but greatly needing my presence & help; and I have still my lands, and some of my property to see after. Yet I lack the means to get home again. The railroads destroyed, the horses & mules carried off, it is only at long intervals that an opportunity offers for travel, and it requires money—which I have not. . . . You have been apprised that I am a widower; that I have lost the one precious companion of 27 years. I have 3 boys & 3 daughters left. Gilmore has had several narrow escapes, & bears the marks of four desperate wounds, & has lost the middle finger of his left hand. . . . Among my losses is my library, 10,700 vols! My books! My books! My heart is ready to break when I think of them. I have had nothing new, in the way of books for four years. My friends here, by the way, the very wealthiest are incapable of helping me, or I should not call upon you & my friends at the North. They have the will, but are as helpless as myself. But enough. I will tell you all, when I am more calm. . . .

Yours Ever as Ever,
W. Gilmore Simms.

3 The 13th Amendment to the Constitution

ABOLITION OF SLAVERY (1865)

AMENDMENT XIII

Section 1.
Neither slavery nor involuntary servitude, except as a punishment for crime whereof the party shall have been duly convicted, shall exist within the United States, or any place subject to their jurisdiction.

Section 2.
Congress shall have power to enforce this article by appropriate legislation.

Passed by Congress January 31, 1865. Ratified December 6, 1865.

Note: A portion of Article IV, section 2, of the Constitution was superseded by the 13th amendment.

4 The 14th Amendment to the Constitution

CIVIL RIGHTS (1868)

AMENDMENT XIV

Section 1.
All persons born or naturalized in the United States, and subject to the jurisdiction thereof, are citizens of the United States and of the State wherein they reside. No State shall make or enforce any law which shall abridge the privileges or immunities of citizens of the United States; nor shall any State deprive any person of life, liberty, or property, without due process of law; nor deny to any person within its jurisdiction the equal protection of the laws.

Section 2.
Representatives shall be apportioned among the several States according to their respective numbers, counting the whole number of persons in each State, excluding Indians not taxed. But when the right to vote at any election for the choice of electors for President and Vice-President of the United States, Representatives in Congress, the Executive and Judicial officers of a State, or the members of the Legislature thereof, is denied to any of the male inhabitants of such State, being twenty-one years of age, and citizens of the United States, or in any way abridged, except for participation in rebellion, or other crime, the basis of representation therein shall be reduced in the proportion which the number of such male citizens shall bear to the whole number of male citizens twenty-one years of age in such State.

Section 3.
No person shall be a Senator or Representative in Congress, or elector of President and Vice-President, or hold any office, civil or military, under the United States, or under any State, who, having previously taken an oath, as a member of Congress, or as an officer of the United States, or as a member of any State legislature, or as an executive or judicial officer of any State, to support the Constitution of the United States, shall have engaged in insurrection or rebellion against the same, or given aid or comfort to the enemies thereof. But Congress may by a vote of two-thirds of each House, remove such disability.

Section 4.
The validity of the public debt of the United States, authorized by law, including debts incurred for payment of pensions and bounties for services in suppressing insurrection or rebellion, shall not be questioned. But neither the United States nor any State shall assume or pay any debt or obligation

incurred in aid of insurrection or rebellion against the United States, or any claim for the loss or emancipation of any slave; but all such debts, obligations and claims shall be held illegal and void.

Section 5.
The Congress shall have the power to enforce, by appropriate legislation, the provisions of this article.

5 The 15th Amendment to the Constitution

VOTING RIGHTS (1870)

Fortieth Congress of the United States of America;

At the third Session, Begun and held at the city of Washington, on Monday, the seventh day of December, one thousand eight hundred and sixty-eight.

A Resolution Proposing an amendment to the Constitution of the United States.

Resolved *by the Senate and House of Respresentatives of the United States of America in Congress assembled*, (two-thirds of both Houses concurring) that the following article be proposed to the legislature of the several States as an amendment to the Constitution of the United States which, when ratified by three-fourths of said legislatures shall be valid as part of the Constitution, namely:

Article XV.

Section 1. The right of citizens of the United States to vote shall not be denied or abridged by the United States or by any State on account of race, color, or previous condition of servitude—

Section 2. The Congress shall have the power to enforce this article by appropriate legislation.

6 “Separate but Equal”: Excerpt from the Supreme Court Ruling in the Case of *Plessy v. Ferguson*, 1896

This case turns upon the constitutionality of an act of the general assembly of the state of Louisiana, passed in 1890, providing for separate railway carriages for the white and colored races. . . .

The constitutionality of this act is attacked upon the ground that it conflicts both with the thirteenth amendment of the Constitution, abolishing slavery, and the fourteenth amendment, which prohibits certain restrictive legislation on the part of the states.

1. That it does not conflict with the thirteenth amendment, which abolished slavery and involuntary servitude, except as a punishment for crime, is too clear for argument. . . .

Indeed, we do not understand that the thirteenth amendment is strenuously relied upon by the plaintiff. . . .

2. . . . The object of the [Fourteenth] amendment was undoubtedly to enforce the absolute equality of the two races before the law, but in the nature of things it could not have been intended to abolish distinctions based upon color, or to enforce social, as distinguished from political, equality, or a commingling of the two races upon terms unsatisfactory to either. Laws permitting, and even requiring, their separation in places where they are liable to be brought into contact do not necessarily imply the inferiority of either race to the other, and have been generally, if not universally, recognized as within the competency of the state legislatures in the exercise of their police power. . . .

So far, then, as a conflict with the fourteenth amendment is concerned, the case reduces itself to the question whether the statute of Louisiana is a reasonable regulation, and with respect to this there must necessarily be a large discretion on the part of the legislature. In determining the question of reasonableness, it is at liberty to act with reference to the established usages, customs, and traditions of the people, and with a view to the promotion of their comfort, and the preservation of the public peace and good order. Gauged by this standard, we cannot say that a law which authorizes or even requires the separation of the two races in public conveyances is unreasonable, or more obnoxious to the fourteenth amendment than the Acts of Congress requiring separate schools for colored children in the District of Columbia, the constitutionality of which does not seem to have been questioned, or the corresponding acts of state legislatures.

We consider the underlying fallacy of the plaintiff's argument to consist in the assumption that the enforced separation of the two races stamps the colored race with a badge of inferiority. If this be so, it is not by reason of anything found in the act, but solely because the colored race chooses to put that construction upon it. . . . The argument also assumes that social prejudices may be overcome by legislation, and that equal rights cannot be secured to the negro except by an enforced commingling of the two races. We cannot accept this proposition. If the two races are to meet upon terms of social equality, it must be the result of natural affinities, a mutual appreciation of each other's merits and a voluntary consent of individuals. . . . Legislation is powerless to eradicate racial instincts or to abolish distinctions based upon physical differences, and the attempt to do so can only result in accentuating the difficulties of the present situation. If the civil and political rights of both races be equal one cannot be inferior to the other civilly or politically. If one race be inferior to the other socially, the Constitution of the United States cannot put them upon the same plane.

7 "Our Constitution Is Color-blind": Excerpt from John Marshall Harlan's Dissenting Opinion in the Case of *Plessy v. Ferguson*, 1896

While there may be in Louisiana persons of different races who are not citizens of the United States, the words in the act 'white and colored races' necessarily include all citizens of the United States of both races residing in that state. So that we have before us a state enactment that compels, under penalties, the separation of the two races in railroad passenger coaches, and makes it a crime for a citizen of either race to enter a coach that has been assigned to citizens of the other race. Thus, the state regulates the use of a public highway by citizens of the United States solely upon the basis of race.

•••

However apparent the injustice of such legislation may be, we have only to consider whether it is consistent with the constitution of the United States.

The thirteenth amendment does not permit the withholding or the deprivation of any right necessarily inhering in freedom. It not only struck down the institution of slavery as previously existing in the United States, but it prevents the imposition of any burdens or disabilities that constitute badges of slavery or servitude. . . . But, that amendment having been found inadequate to the protection of the rights of those who had been in slavery, it was followed by the fourteenth amendment . . . declaring that 'all persons born or naturalized in the United States, and subject to the jurisdiction thereof, are citizens of the United States and of the state wherein they reside,' and that 'no state shall make or enforce any law which shall abridge the privileges or immunities of citizens of the United States; nor shall any state deprive any person of life, liberty or property without due process of law, nor deny to any person within its jurisdiction the equal protection of the laws.' These two amendments [Thirteenth and Fourteenth], if enforced according to their true intent and meaning, will protect all the civil rights that pertain to freedom and citizenship.

•••

The white race deems itself to be the dominant race in this country. And so it is, in prestige, in achievements, in education, in wealth, and in power. So, I doubt not, it will continue to be for all time, if it remains true to its great heritage, and holds fast to the principles of constitutional liberty. But in view of the constitution, in the eye of the law, there is in this country no superior, dominant, ruling class of citizens. There is no caste here. Our constitution is color-blind, and neither knows nor tolerates classes among citizens. In respect of civil rights, all citizens are equal before the law.

. . . The present decision, it may well be apprehended, will not only stimulate aggressions, more or less brutal and irritating, upon the admitted rights of colored citizens, but will encourage the belief that it is possible, by means of state enactments, to defeat the beneficient purposes which the people of the United States had in view when they adopted the recent amendments of the constitution, by one of which the blacks of this country were made citizens of the United States and of the states in which they respectively reside, and whose privileges and immunities, as citizens, the states are forbidden to abridge. Sixty millions of whites are in no danger from the presence here of eight millions of blacks. The destinies of the two races, in this country, are indissolubly linked together, and the interests of both require that the common government of all shall not permit the seeds of race hate to be planted under the sanction of law. What can more certainly arouse race hate, what more certainly create and perpetuate a feeling of distrust between these races, than state enactments which, in fact, proceed on the ground that colored citizens are so inferior and degraded that they cannot be allowed to sit in public coaches occupied by white citizens? That, as all will admit, is the real meaning of such legislation as was enacted in Louisiana.

8 Ida B. Wells Explores Lynching: Excerpt from "Lynch Law in America," 1900

Our country's national crime is *lynching*. It is not the creature of an hour, the sudden outburst of uncontrolled fury, or the unspeakable brutality of an insane mob. It represents the cool, calculating deliberation of an intelligent people who openly avow that there is an "unwritten law" that justifies them in putting to death without complaint under oath, without trial by jury, without opportunity to make defense, without right of appeal. . . .

The alleged menace of universal suffrage having been avoided by the absolute suppression of the negro vote, the spirit of mob murder should have been satisfied and the butchery of negroes should have ceased. But men, women, and children were the victims of murder by individuals and murder by mobs, just as they had been when killed at the demands of the "unwritten law" to prevent "negro domination." Negroes were killed for disputing over terms of contracts with their employers. If a few barns were burned some colored man was killed to stop it. If a colored man resented the imposition of a white man and the two come to blows, the colored man had to die, either at the hands of the white man then and there or later at the hands of the mob that speedily gathered. If he showed a spirit of courageous manhood he was hanged for his pains, and the killing was justified by the declaration that he was a "saucy nigger." Colored women have been murdered because they refused to tell the mobs where relatives could be found for "lynching bees." Boys of fourteen years have been lynched by white representatives of American civilization. In fact, for all kinds of offenses—and for no offenses—from murders to misdemeanors, men and women are put to death without judge or jury; so that, although the political excuse was no longer necessary, the wholesale murder of human beings went on just the same. A new name was given to the killings and a new excuse was invented for doing so.

Again the aid of the "unwritten law" is invoked, and again it comes to the rescue. During the last ten years a new statute has been added to the "unwritten law." This statute proclaims that for certain crimes or alleged crimes no negro shall be allowed a trial; that no white woman shall be compelled to charge an assault under oath or to submit any such charge to the investigation of a court of law. The result is that many men have been put to death whose innocence was afterward established; and today, under the reign of the "unwritten law," no colored man, no matter what his reputation, is safe from lynching if a white woman, no matter what her standing or motive, cares to charge him with insult or assault.

It is considered a sufficient excuse and reasonable justification to put a prisoner to death under this "unwritten law" for the frequently repeated charge that these lynching horrors are necessary to prevent crimes against women. The sentiment of the country has been appealed to, in describing the isolated condition of white families in thickly populated negro districts;

and the charge is made that these homes are in as great danger as if they were surrounded by wild beasts. And the world has accepted this theory without let or hindrance. In many cases there has been open expression that the fate meted out to the victim was only what he deserved. In many other instances there has been a silence that says more forcibly than words can proclaim it that it is right and proper that a human being should be seized by a mob and burned to death upon the unsworn and the uncorroborated charge of his accuser. No matter that our laws presume every man innocent until he is proved guilty; no matter that it encourages those criminally disposed to blacken their faces and commit any crime in the calendar so long as they can throw suspicion on some negro as is frequently done, and then lead a mob to take his life; no matter that mobs make a farce of the law and a mockery of justice; no matter that hundreds of boys are being hardened in crime and schooled in vice by the repetition of such scenes before their eyes—if a white woman declares herself insulted or assaulted, some life must pay the penalty, with all the horrors of the Spanish Inquisition and all the barbarism of the Middle Ages. The world looks on and says it is well.

•••

Quite a number of the one-third alleged cases of assault that have been personally investigated by the writer have shown that there was no foundation in fact for the charges; yet the claim is not made that there were no real culprits among them. The negro has been too long associated with the white man not to have copied his vices as well as his virtues. But the negro resents and utterly repudiates the effort to blacken his good name by asserting that assaults suffered far more from the commission of this crime against the women of his race by white men than the white race has ever suffered through his crimes. Very scant notice is taken of the matter when this is the condition of affairs. What becomes a crime deserving capital punishment when the tables are turned is a matter of small moment when the negro woman is the accusing party. . . .

Section 2

Industrialization, Reform, and the Coming of War, 1880s–1920

1 Jay Gould Testifies on the Relations Between Bosses and Laborers, 1883

Senator Blair: We have had a man six feet high, who has driven a truck team, and who has more intellectual capacity than half, or perhaps any, of the members of Congress, offering here before this committee to agree under contract to work diligently and faithfully for the next twenty years for anybody who would give him employment and agree to maintain himself and his family. That man said he had been unable to get anything ahead, and could not find a chance to work; that he was hungry, and his family were hungry, and that he didn't know what to do; and it was represented to us here that he was one of a large class. He said that folks told him to go West; but such a man cannot go West, if he tells the truth about his situation, and even if he were to adopt the plan you suggest, his family certainly could not accompany him, driving a mule on the canal tow-path. . . .

Jay Gould: Well, I know there are a great many cases of actual suffering in a large city like this, and in all large cities. It is a very difficult thing to say exactly how you are to everybody's condition. I have noticed, though, that generally if men are temperate and industrious they are pretty sure of success. In cases such as the one you describe I could almost always go back behind the scenes and find a cause for such a person's "misfortunes."

Blair: There has been testimony before us that the feeling generally between employers and employees throughout the country is one of hostility, especially on the part of the employees toward those whom they designate as monopolists. From your observation, what do you think is really the feeling as a general rule between those two classes?

Gould: I think that if left alone they would mutually regulate their relations. I think there is no disagreement between the great mass of the employees and their employers. These societies that are gotten up magnify these things and create evils which do not exist—create trouble which ought not to exist.

Blair: Of the men who conduct business enterprises and wield the power of capital in this country today, what proportion do you think are what are called "self-made men"?

Gould: I think they are all "self-made men"; I do not say self-made exactly, for the country has grown and they have grown up with it. In this country we have no system of heirlooms or of handing down estates. Every man has to stand here on his own individual merit.

Blair: What is the proportion of those men who have made their own fortunes pecuniarily, such as they are?

U.S. Congress, Senate, *Report of the Senate Committee upon the Relations between Labor and Capital* (Washington, D.C.: Government Printing Office, 1885), 47–133.

Gould: I think they are nearly all of that class. I think, that according to my observation in the field that I have been in, nearly every one that occupies a prominent position has come up from the ranks, worked his own way along up. . . .

Blair: . . . Won't you please give us, . . . as fully as you see fit . . . your idea in regard to the establishment of a postal telegraph for the purpose of supplanting or rivaling the existing telegraphic systems of the country now controlled by private ownership?

Gould: Well, I think that control by the government in such things is contrary to our institutions. A telegraph system, of all businesses in the world, wants to be managed by skilled experts. Our government is founded on a political idea; that is, that the party in power shall control the patronage; and if the government controlled the telegraph, the heads of the general managers and the superintendents would come off every four years, if there was a change in politics—at least as often as that—and you would not have any such efficient service as you have now. The very dividend of the Western Union depends upon the company doing the business well, keeping her customers, and developing the business. But if the government controlled it—why if the Democrats were in power it would be a Democratic telegraph, and if the Republicans came into power it would be a Republican telegraph, and if the great Reformers came in I don't know what they would do with it. I think they would —

Blair: [Interposing.] It will not be very important to decide that until they come in.

Gould: No, sir. . . .

Blair: Would you regard a corporate property like that of the Western Union, which is based upon a franchise to which the public are a party, as standing upon the same ground with reference to its right to create an increase of earning power that a piece of private property stands upon where there is no franchise obtained from the public?

Gould: I look upon corporate property in this way. I make a great difference between corporate property and private property. Corporate property is clothed with public rights and has duties to the public, and I regard those duties as paramount, really, to the rights of the stockholders. A corporation has first to perform its public obligations and the business that it was created to do; but when you have gone to that extent, then beyond that, I put it upon the same ground as private property. I judge of its value by its net earning power, the same as I judge of any private property; because I have faith in the government—I have faith in the republican institutions under which we live.

Blair: Right upon that point, is one of those public rights of which you speak—the right to exercise the power of reducing, regulating, or controlling the charges which the corporation may make for the services which it renders to the public and for which the public pays.

Gould: They can regulate those charges within the limits of legislative direction. For instance, if the legislature should come in and fix a limit, that becomes the law of the corporation. The legislature can regulate the rates to be imposed. That is the great hold of the public upon corporations. If unreasonable rates are established or unreasonable regulations made by a corporation, the legislature can come in and control them, and its directions are paramount. For instance, if there was a great clamor that the Western Union Company was charging unreasonable rates, it would be perfectly fair for the legislature to come in and examine into that question, and if they found the rates or regulations unreasonable, to control them by legislative action. Their control is paramount to every other control. But that would be a very different thing from the government going into the business of telegraphing and destroying the property of her own citizens. . . .

Blair: Do you think there would be any opposition made to a general national law regulating the fares and freight charges upon interstate commerce?

Gould: Well, I don't know about that. I think the freer you allow things to be the better. They regulate themselves. The laws of supply and demand, production and consumption, enter into and settle those matters. . . . I know that some years ago, when I was connected with the Chicago and Northwestern road, the states of Wisconsin and some of the other states passed what were called the "Granger laws"; but they repealed them afterwards, because they found on practical investigation that that legislation was tending to frighten capital away from those states, and to retard their development. Finding that to be so, in order to bring back confidence they repealed the laws and left the roads free to work out their own success. . . .

A corporation is only another name for the means which we have discovered of allowing a poor man to invest his income in a great enterprise. In other words, instead of one man owning any of these great properties in bulk, they are divided into small shares, so that the man who has got only $200 or $500 or $5,000, or whatever it may be, can own an interest in proportion to his capital. That is what a corporation means.

Blair: Then, in your opinion, the natural operation of the laws of descent as they exist in this country is to guard the community against any danger from the perpetuation of associated corporate wealth, or of great individual fortunes in the future?

Gould: Yes, sir; I do not think there is any need to be afraid of capital; capital is [not] scary. What you have got to fear is large, ignorant masses of population; I don't think the liberties of the people have anything to fear from capital. Capital is conservative and scary; but what you have to fear in a republican government like ours, where there is no military control, is large masses of uneducated, ignorant people.

Blair: Do you think there is any danger to this country in that direction?

Gould: I think we are accumulating great masses of such people from abroad. Whether we have a system that will educate them up rapidly enough I do not know.

Blair: If there was to be any legislation in any direction on this general question, don't you think that it might as well be in the direction of educating the people as in any other?

Gould: I think that is what we should do—educate the masses, elevate their moral standards. I think that is the only protection we can have for a long period in the future. When the people are educated and intelligent you have nothing to fear from them.

Blair: Do you think that to do that would accomplish more for labor than anything else we could do?

Gould: Yes, sir; because education fits a man so that if he does not like one field of labor he can go to another. Business is constantly changing, and where there is an excess of one class of labor there is very likely to be a lack of another class, and if a man is properly educated he can turn his hand to a great many different things. . . .

Blair: Do you think that the large employers of labor, the manufacturing corporations, the transportation companies, the telegraph companies, and so on, and also individuals who employ help in large masses and who necessarily classify their help, paying them different rates of wages, according to classes rather than according to their individual merits do you think that they might profitably ingraft upon their business some system of assurance, or some method by which a portion of the earnings of the laborers should be contributed to a fund, and perhaps a proportion of the profit of capital also, to secure the working people against want in seasons of nonemployment, and against the disabilities resulting from accident, sickness, or old age? Could something of that kind be introduced which would be of benefit to the laboring people?

Gould: The trouble about that is that the drones would get control of the money and spend it, in nine cases out of ten. It is a good thing in theory, but I fear it would not work well in practice.

2 Thomas O'Donnell Testifies on the Conditions of Labor, 1887

THOMAS O'DONNELL
TESTIMONY BEFORE A U.S. SENATE COMMITTEE, 1885

Senator Blair: Are you a married man?

Thomas O'Donnell: Yes, sir; I am a married man; have a wife and two children. I am not very well educated. I went to work when I was young, and have been working ever since in the cotton business; went to work when I was about eight or nine years old. I was going to state how I live. My children get along very well in summer time, on account of not having to buy fuel or shoes or one thing and another. I earn $1.50 a day and can't afford to pay a very big house rent. I pay $1.50 a week for rent, which comes to about $6.00 a month.

Blair: That is, you pay this where you are at Fall River?

O'Donnell: Yes, Sir.

Blair: Do you have work right along?

O'Donnell: No, sir; since that strike we had down in Fall River about three years ago I have not worked much more than half the time, and that has brought my circumstances down very much.

Blair: Why have you not worked more than half the time since then?

O'Donnell: Well, at Fall River if a man has not got a boy to act as "backboy" it is very hard for him to get along. In a great many cases they discharge men in that work and put in men who have boys.

Blair: Men who have boys of their own?

O'Donnell: Men who have boys of their own capable enough to work in a mill, to earn $.30 or $.40 a day.

Blair: Is the object of that to enable the boy to earn something for himself?

O'Donnell: Well, no; the object is this: They are doing away with a great deal of mule-spinning there and putting in ring-spinning, and for that reason it takes a good deal of small help to run this ring work, and it throws the men out of work. . . . For that reason they get all the small help they can to run these ring-frames. There are so many men in the city to work, and whoever has a boy can have work, and whoever has no boy stands no chance. Probably he may have a few months of work in the summer time, but will be discharged

---

U.S. Congress, Senate, *Report of the Senate Committee upon the Relations between Labor and Capital* (Washington, D.C.: Government Printing Office, 1885).

in the fall. That is what leaves me in poor circumstances. Our children, of course, are very often sickly from one cause or another, on account of not having sufficient clothes, or shoes, or food, or something. And also my woman; she never did work in a mill; she was a housekeeper, and for that reason she can't help me to anything at present, as many women do help their husbands down there, by working, like themselves. . . .

Blair: How much [work] have you had within a year?

O'Donnell: Since Thanksgiving I happened to get work in the Crescent Mill, and worked there exactly thirteen weeks. I got just $1.50 a day, with the exception of a few days that I lost because in following up mule-spinning you are obliged to lose a day once in a while; you can't follow it up regularly.

Blair: Thirteen weeks would be seventy-eight days, and, at $1.50 a day, that would make $117, less whatever time you lost?

O'Donnell: Yes. I worked thirteen weeks there and ten days in another place, and then there was a dollar I got this week, Wednesday.

Blair: Taking a full year back can you tell how much you have had?

O'Donnell: That would be about fifteen weeks' work. . . .

Blair: That would be somewhere about $133, if you had not lost any time?

O'Donnell: Yes, sir.

Blair: That is all you have had?

O'Donnell: Yes, sir.

Blair: To support yourself and wife and two children?

O'Donnell: Yes, sir.

Blair: Have you had any help from outside?

O'Donnell: No, sir.

Blair: Do you mean that yourself and wife and two children have had nothing but that for all this time?

O'Donnell: That is all. I got a couple dollars' worth of coal last winter, and the wood I picked up myself. I goes around with a shovel and picks up clams and wood.

Blair: What do you do with the clams?

O'Donnell: We eat them. I don't get them to sell, but just to eat, for the family. That is the way my brother lives, too, mostly. He lives close by us.

Blair: How many live in that way down there?

O'Donnell: I could not count them, they are so numerous. I suppose there are one thousand down there.

Blair: A thousand that live on $150 a year?

O'Donnell: They live on less.

Blair: Less than that?

O'Donnell: Yes; they live on less than I do.

Blair: How long has that been so?

O'Donnell: Mostly so since I have been married.

Blair: How long is that?

O'Donnell: Six years this month.

Blair: Why do you not go West on a farm?

O'Donnell: How could I go, walk it?

Blair: Well, I want to know why you do not go out West on a $2,000 farm, or take up a homestead and break it and work it up, and then have it for yourself and family?

O'Donnell: I can't see how I could get out West. I have got nothing to go with.

Blair: It would not cost you over $1,500.

O'Donnell: Well, I never saw over a $20 bill, and that is when I have been getting a month's pay at once. If someone would give me $1,500 I will go. . . .

Blair: Are you a good workman?

O'Donnell: Yes, sir.

Blair: Were you ever turned off because of misconduct or incapacity or unfitness for work?

O'Donnell: No, sir.

Blair: Or because you did bad work?

O'Donnell: No, sir.

Blair: Or because you made trouble among the help?

O'Donnell: No, sir. . . .

Blair: How old are you?

O'Donnell: About thirty.

Blair: Is your health good?

O'Donnell: Yes, sir.

Blair: What would you work for if you could get work right along; if you could be sure to have it for five years, staying right where you are?

O'Donnell: Well, if I was where my family could be with me, and I could have work every day I would take $1.50, and be glad to. . . .

Blair: You spoke of fuel—what do you have for fuel?

O'Donnell: Wood and coal.

Blair: Where does the wood come from?

O'Donnell: I pick it up around the shore—any old pieces I see around that are not good for anything. There are many more that do the same thing.

Blair: Do you get meat to live on much?

O'Donnell: Very seldom.

Blair: What kinds of meat do you get for your family?

O'Donnell: Well, once in a while we get a piece of pork and some clams and make a clam chowder. That makes a very good meal. We sometimes get a piece of corn beef or something like that. . . .

Blair: What have you eaten?

O'Donnell: Well, bread mostly, when we could get it; we sometimes couldn't make out to get that, and have had to go without a meal.

Blair: Has there been any day in the year that you have had to go without anything to eat?

O'Donnell: Yes, sir, several days.

Blair: More than one day at a time?

O'Donnell: No. . . .

Blair: What have the children got on in the way of clothing?

O'Donnell: They have got along very nicely all summer, but now they are beginning to feel quite sickly. One has one shoe on, a very poor one, and a slipper, that was picked up somewhere. The other has two odd shoes on, with the heel out. He has got cold and is sickly now.

Blair: Have they any stockings?

O'Donnell: He had got stockings, but his feet comes through them, for there is a hole in the bottom of the shoe.

Blair: What have they got on the rest of their person?

O'Donnell: Well, they have a little calico shirt—what should be a shirt; it is sewed up in some shape—and one little petticoat, and a kind of little dress.

Blair: How many dresses has your wife got?

O'Donnell: She has got one since she was married, and she hasn't worn that more than half a dozen times; she has worn it just going to church and coming back. She is very good in going to church, but when she comes back she takes it off, and it is pretty near as good now as when she bought it.

Blair: She keeps that dress to go to church in?

O'Donnell: Yes, sir.

Blair: How many dresses aside from that has she?

O'Donnell: Well, she got one here three months ago.

Blair: What did it cost?

O'Donnell: It cost $1.00 to make it and I guess about a dollar for the stuff, as near as I can tell . . . she has an undershirt that she got given to her, and she has an old wrapper, which is about a mile too big for her; somebody gave it to her. . . . That is all that I know that she has. . . .

Blair: Do you see any way out of your troubles—what are you going to do for a living—or do you expect to have to stay right there?

O'Donnell: Yes. I can't run around with my family.

Blair: You have nowhere to go to, and no way of getting there if there was any place to go to?

O'Donnell: No, sir; I have no means nor anything, so I am obliged to remain there and try to pick up something as I can.

Blair: Do the children go to school?

O'Donnell: No, sir; they are not old enough; the oldest child is only three and a half; the youngest one is one and a half years old.

Blair: Is there anything else you wanted to say?

O'Donnell: Nothing further, except that I would like some remedy to be got to help us poor people down there in some way. Excepting the government decides to do something with us we have a poor show. We are all, or mostly all, in good health; that is, as far as the men who are at work go.

Blair: You do not know anything but mule-spinning, I suppose?

O'Donnell: That is what I have been doing, but I sometimes do something with pick and shovel. I have worked for a man at that, because I am so put on. I am looking for work in a mill. The way they do there is this: There are about twelve or thirteen men that go into a mill every morning, and they have to stand their chance, looking for work. The man who has a boy with him he stands the best chance, and then, if it is my turn or a neighbor's turn who has no boy, if another man comes in who has a boy he is taken right in, and we are left out. I said to the boss once it was my turn to go in, and now you have taken on that man; what am I to do; I have got two little boys at home, one of them three years and a half and the other one year and a half old, and how am I to find something for them to eat; I can't get my turn when I come here. He said he could not do anything for me. I says, "Have I got to starve; ain't I to have any work?" They are forcing these young boys into the mills that should not be in mills at all; forcing them in because they are throwing the mules out and putting on ring-frames. They are doing everything of that kind that they possibly can to crush down the poor people—the poor operatives there.

3 John Rockefeller Testifies on the Practices of "Big Business," 1899

TESTIMONY TO THE U.S. INDUSTRIAL COMMISSION, 1899

Q. Did the Standard Oil Company or other affiliated interests at any time before 1887 receive from the railroads rebates on freight shipped, or other special advantages?

A. The Standard Oil Company of Ohio, of which I was president, did receive rebates from the railroads prior to 1880, but received no special advantages for which it did not give full compensation. The reason for rebates was that such was the railroads' method of business. A public rate was made and collected by the railway companies, but so far as my knowledge extends, was never really retained in full, a portion of it was repaid to the shippers as a rebate. By this method the real rate of freight which any shipper paid was not known by his competitors nor by other railway companies, the amount being in all cases a matter of bargain with the carrying company. Each shipper made the best bargain he could, but whether he was doing better than his competitor was only a matter of conjecture. Much depended upon whether the shipper had the advantage of competition of carriers. The Standard Oil Company of Ohio, being situated at Cleveland, had the advantage of different carrying lines, as well as of water transportation in the summer, and taking advantage of those facilities made the best bargains possible for its freights. All the other companies did the same, their success depending largely upon whether they had the choice of more than one route. The Standard sought also to offer advantages to the railways for the purpose of lessening rates of freight. It offered freights in large quantity, carloads and trainloads. It furnished loading facilities and discharging facilities. It exempted railways from liability for fire. For these services it obtained contracts for special allowances on freights. These never exceeded, to the best of my personal recollections, 10 per cent. But in almost every instance it was discovered subsequently that our competitors had been obtaining as good, and, in some instances, better rates of freight than ourselves. . . .

Q. About what percentage of the profits of the Standard Oil Company came from special advantages given by the railroads. . . .

A. No percentage of the profits of the Standard Oil Company came from advantages given by railroads at any time. Whatever advantage it received in its constant efforts to reduce rates of freight was deducted from the price of oil.

U.S. Industrial Commission, *Preliminary Report on Trusts and Industrial Combinations*, 56th Congress, 1st Session (December 30, 1899), Document No. 476, Part 1, 794–97.

The advantages to the Standard from low freight rates consisted solely in the increased volume of its business arising from the low price of its products. . . .

Q. Has the Standard Oil Company received any financial favors from any railroad since 1887?

A. To my knowledge, none whatever.

Q. Has the ownership of stock in railroad companies by officers of the Standard Oil Company given the Standard advantages with those railroads over its competitors?. . . .

A. It has not. Stockholders and officers of the Standard have invested in stock of railway companies. But in no instance have they done so for the purpose of influencing the policy of the railway companies, nor to the best of my knowledge and belief has any attempt ever been made through such ownership to influence any railway in favor of the Standard.

Q. To what advantages, or favors, or methods of management do you ascribe chiefly the success of the Standard Oil Company?

A. I ascribe the success of the Standard to its consistent policy to make the volume of its business large through the merits and cheapness of its products. It has spared no expense in finding, securing, and utilizing the best and cheapest methods of manufacture. It has sought for the best superintendents and workmen and paid the best wages. It has not hesitated to sacrifice old machinery and old plants for new and better ones. It has placed its manufactories at the points where they could supply markets at the least expense. It has not only sought markets for its principal products, but for all possible by-products, sparing no expense in introducing them to the public. It has not hesitated to invest millions of dollars in methods for cheapening the gathering and distribution of oils by pipe lines, special cars, tank steamers, and tank wagons. It has erected tank stations at every important railroad station to cheapen the storage and delivery of its products. It has spared no expense in forcing its products into the markets of the world among people civilized and uncivilized. It has had faith in American oil, and has brought together millions of money for the purpose of making it what it is, and holding its markets against the competition of Russia and all the many countries which are producers of oil and competitors against American oil.

Q. What are, in your judgment, the chief advantages from industrial combinations (a) financially to stockholders; (b) to the public?

A. All the advantages which can be derived from a cooperation of persons and aggregation of capital. Much that one man can not do alone two can do together, and once admit the fact that cooperation, or, what is the same thing, combination, is necessary on a small scale, the limit depends solely upon the necessities of business. Two persons in partnership may be a sufficiently large combination for a small business, but if the business grows or can be made to grow, more persons and more capital must be taken in. The business may grow so large that a partnership ceases to be a proper instrumentality for its purposes, and then a corporation becomes a necessity. In most countries, as in England, this form of industrial combination is sufficient for a business coextensive with the parent country, but it is not so in this country. Our Federal form of government making every corporation created by a State foreign to every other State, renders it necessary for persons doing business through corporate agency to organize corporations in some or many of the different States in which their business is located. Instead of doing business through the agency of one corporation they must do business through the agencies of several corporations. If the business is extended to foreign countries, and Americans are not today satisfied with home markets alone, it will be found helpful and possibly necessary to organize corporations in such countries, for Europeans are prejudiced against foreign corporations as are the people of many of our States. These different corporations thus become cooperating agencies in the same business and are held together by common ownership of their stocks.

It is too late to argue about the advantages of industrial combinations. They are a necessity. And if Americans are to have the privilege of extending their business in all the States of the Union, and into foreign countries as well, they are a necessity on a large scale, and require the agency of more than one corporation. Their chief advantages are:

(1) Command of necessary capital.
(2) Extension of limits of business.
(3) Increase of number of persons interested in the business.
(4) Economy in the business.
(5) Improvements and economies which are derived from knowledge of many interested persons of wide experience.
(6) Power to give the public improved products at less prices and still make profit for stockholders.
(7) Permanent work and good wages for laborers.

I speak from my experience in the business with which I have been intimately connected for about 40 years. Our first combination was a partnership and afterwards a corporation in Ohio. That was sufficient for a local refining business. But dependent solely upon local business we should have failed years ago. We were forced to extend our markets and to seek for export trade. This latter made the seaboard cities a necessary place of business, and we soon discovered that manufacturing for export could be more economically carried on at the seaboard, hence refineries at Brooklyn, at Bayonne, at Philadelphia, and necessary corporations in New York, New Jersey, and Pennsylvania.

We soon discovered as the business grew that the primary method of transporting oil in barrels could not last. The package often cost more than the contents and the forests of the country were not sufficient to supply the necessary material for an extended length of time. Hence we devoted attention to other methods of transportation, adopted the pipe-line system, and found capital for pipe-line construction equal to the necessities of the business.

To operate pipe lines required francluses from the States in which they were located, and consequently corporations in those States, just as railroads running through different States, are forced to operate under separate State charters. To perfect the pipe-line system of transportation required in the neighborhood of fifty millions of capital. This could not be obtained or maintained without industrial combination. The entire oil business is dependent upon this pipe-line system. Without it every well would shut down and every foreign market could be closed to us.

The pipe-line system required other improvements, such as tank cars upon railways, and finally the tank steamer. Capital had to be furnished for them and corporations created to own and operate them.

Every step taken was necessary in the business if it was to be properly developed, and only through such successive steps and by such an industrial combination is America today enabled to utilize the bounty which its land pours forth, and to furnish the world with the best and cheapest light ever known, receiving in return . . . from foreign lands nearly $50,000,000 per year, most of which is distributed in payment of American labor.

I have given a picture rather than a detail of the growth of one industrial combination. It is a pioneer, and its work has been of incalculable value. There are other American products besides oil for which the markets of the world can be opened, and legislators will be blind to our best industrial interests if they unduly hinder by legislation the combination of persons and capital requisite for the attainment of so desirable an end.

Q. What are the chief disadvantages or dangers to the public arising from them?

A. The dangers are that the power conferred by combination may be abused; that combinations may be formed for speculation in stocks rather than for conducting business, and that for this purpose prices may be temporarily raised instead of being lowered. These abuses are possible to a greater or less extent in all combinations, large or small, but this fact is no more of an argument against combinations than the fact that steam may explode is an argument against steam. Steam is necessary and can be made comparatively safe. Combination is necessary and its abuses can be minimized; otherwise our legislators must acknowledge their incapacity to deal with the most important instrument of industry. Hitherto most legislative attempts have been an effort not to control but to destroy; hence their futility.

4 The Interstate Commerce Act, 1887

Forty-Ninth Congress of the United States of America;

At the Second Session,
Begun and held at the City of Washington on Monday, the sixth day of December, one thousand eight hundred and eighty-six

An act to regulate Commerce.

Be it enacted by the Senate and House of Representatives of the United States of America in Congress assembled, That the provisions of this act shall apply to any common carrier or carriers engaged in the transportation of passengers or property wholly by railroad, or partly by railroad and partly by water when both are used, under a common control, management, or arrangement, for a continuous carriage or shipment, from one State or Territory of the United States, or the District of Columbia, to any other State or Territory of the United States, or the District of Columbia, or from any place in the United States to an adjacent foreign country, or from any place in the United States through a foreign country to any other place in the United States, and also to the transportation in like manner of property shipped from any place in the United States to a foreign country and carried from such place to a port of trans-shipment, or shipped from a foreign country to any place in the United States and carried to such place from a port of entry either in the United States or an adjacent foreign country: *Provided, however*, That the provisions of this act shall not apply to the transportation of passengers or property, or to the receiving, delivering, storage, or handling of property, wholly within one State, and not shipped to or from a foreign country from or to any State or Territory as aforesaid.

The term "railroad" as used in this act shall include all bridges and ferries used or operated in connection with any railroad, and also all the road in use by any corporation operating a railroad, whether owned or operated under a contract, agreement, or lease; and the term "transportation" shall include all instrumentalities of shipment or carriage.

All charges made for any service rendered or to be rendered in the transportation of passengers or property as aforesaid, or in connection therewith, or for the receiving, delivering, storage, or handling of such property, shall be reasonable and just; and every unjust and unreasonable charge for such service is prohibited and declared to be unlawful.

Sec. 2. That if any common carrier subject to the provisions of this act shall, directly or indirectly, by any special rate, rebate, drawback, or other device, charge, demand, collect, or receive from any person or persons a greater or less compensation for any service rendered, or to be rendered, in the transportation of passengers or property, subject to the provisions of this act, than it charges, demands, collects, or receives from any other person or persons for doing for him or them a like and contemporaneous service in the transportation of a like kind of traffic under substantially similar circumstances and conditions, such common carrier shall be deemed guilty of unjust discrimination, which is hereby prohibited and declared to be unlawful.

Sec. 3. That it shall be unlawful for any common carrier subject to the provisions of this act to make or give any undue or unreasonable preference or advantage to any particular person, company, firm, corporation, or locality, or any particular description of traffic, in any respect whatsoever, or to subject any particular person, company, firm, corporation, or locality, or any particular description of traffic, to any undue or unreasonable prejudice or disadvantage in any respect whatsoever.

Every common carrier subject to the provisions of this act shall according to their respective powers, afford all reasonable, proper, and equal facilities for the interchange of traffic between their respective lines, and for the receiving, forwarding, and delivering of passengers and property to and from their several lines and those connection therewith, and shall not discriminate in their rates and charges between such connecting lines; but this shall not be construed as requiring any such common carrier to give the use of its tracks or terminal facilities to another carrier engaged in like business.

Sec. 4. That it shall be unlawful for any common carrier subject to the provisions of this act to charge or receive any greater compensation in the aggregate for the transportation of passengers or of like kind of property, under substantially similar circumstances and conditions, for a shorter than for a longer distance over the same line, in the same direction, the shorter being included within the longer distance; but this shall not be construed as authorizing any common carrier within the terms of this act to charge and receive as great compensation for a shorter as for a longer distance: *Provided, however*, That upon application to the Commission appointed under the provisions of this act, such common carrier may, in special cases, after investigation by the Commission, be authorized to charge less for longer than for shorter distances for the transportation of passengers or property; and the Commission may from time to time prescribe the extent to which such designated common carrier may be relieved from the operation of this section of this act.

Sec. 5. That it shall be unlawful for any common carrier subject to the provisions of this act to enter into any contract, agreement, or combination with any other common carrier or carriers for the pooling of freights of different and competing railroads, or to divide between them the aggregate or net proceeds of the earnings of such railroads, or any portion thereof; and in any case of an agreement for the pooling of freights as aforesaid, each day of its continuance shall be deemed a separate offense.

Sec. 6. That every common carrier subject to the provisions of this act shall print and keep for public inspection schedules showing the rates and fares and charges for the transportation of passengers and property which any such common carrier has established and which are in force at the time upon its railroad, as defined by the first section of this act. The schedules printed as aforesaid by any such common carrier shall plainly state the places upon its railroad between which property and passengers will be carried, and shall contain the classification of freight in force upon such railroad, and shall also state separately the terminal charges and any rules or regulations which in any wise change, affect, or determine any part or the aggregate of such aforesaid rates and fares and charges. Such schedules shall be plainly printed in large type, of at least the size of ordinary pica, and copies for the use of the public shall be kept in every depot or station upon any such railroad, in such places and in such form that they can be conveniently inspected.

And when any such common carrier shall have established and published its rates, fares, and charges in compliance with the provisions of this section, it shall be unlawful for such common carrier to charge, demand, collect, or receive from any person or persons a greater or less compensation for the transportation of passengers or property, or for any services in connection therewith, than is specified in such published schedule of rates, fares, and charges as may at the time be in force.

Sec. 7. That it shall be unlawful for any common carrier subject to the provisions of this act to enter into any combination, contract, or agreement, expressed or implied, to prevent, by change of time schedule, carriage in different cars, or by other means or devices, the carriage of freights from being continuous from the place of shipment to the place of destination; and no break of bulk, stoppage, or interruption made by such common carrier shall prevent the carriage of freights from being and being treated as one continuous carriage from the place of shipment to the place of destination, unless such break, stoppage, or interruption was made in good faith for some necessary purpose, and without any intent to avoid or unnecessarily interrupt such continuous carriage or to evade any of the provisions of this act.

Sec. 8. That in case any common carrier subject to the provisions of this act shall do, cause to be done, or permit to be done any act, matter, or thing in this act prohibited or declared to be unlawful, or shall omit to do any act, matter, or thing in this act required to be done, such common carrier shall be liable to the person or persons injured thereby for the full amount of damages sustained in consequence of any such violation of the provisions of this act, together with a reasonable counsel or attorney's fee, to be fixed by the court in every case of recovery, which attorney's fee shall be taxed and collected as part of the costs in the case.

Sec. 10. That any common carrier subject to the provisions of this act, or, whenever such common carrier is a corporation, any director or officer thereof, or any receiver, trustee, lessee, agent, or person acting for or employed by such corporation, who, alone or with any other corporation, company, person, or party, shall willfully do or cause to be done, or shall willingly suffer or permit to be done, any act, matter, or thing in this act prohibited or declared to be unlawful, or who shall aid or abet therein, or shall willfully omit or fail to do any act, matter, or thing in this act required to be done, or shall cause or willingly suffer or permit any act, matter, or thing so directed or required by this act to be done not to be so done, or shall aid or abet any such omission or failure, or shall be guilty of any infraction of this act, or shall aid or abet therein, shall be deemed guilty of a misdemeanor, and shall, upon conviction thereof in any district court of the United States within the jurisdiction of which such offense was committed, be subject to a fine of not to exceed five thousand dollars for each offense.

Sec. 11. That a Commission is hereby created and established to be known as the Inter-State Commerce Commission, which shall be composed of five Commissioners, who shall be appointed by the President, by and with the advice and consent of the Senate. The Commissioners first appointed under this act shall continue in office for the term of two, three, four, five, and six years, respectively, from the first day of January, anno Domini eighteen hundred and eighty-seven, the term of each to be designated by the President; but their successors shall be appointed for terms of six years, except that any person chosen to fill a vacancy shall be appointed only for the unexpired term of the Commissioner whom he shall succeed. Any Commissioner may be removed by the President for inefficiency, neglect of duty, or malfeasance in office. Not more than three of the Commissioners shall be appointed from the same political party. No person in the employ of or holding any official relation to any common carrier subject to the provisions of this act, or owning stock or bonds thereof, or who is in any manner pecuniarily interested therein, shall enter upon the duties of or hold such office. Said Commissioners shall not engage in any other business, vocation, or employment.

No vacancy in the Commission shall impair the right of the remaining Commissioners to exercise all the powers of the Commission.

Sec. 12. That the Commission hereby created shall have authority to inquire into the management of the business of all common carriers subject to the provisions of this act, and shall keep itself informed as to the manner and method in which the same is conducted, and shall have the right to obtain from such common carriers full and complete information necessary to enable the Commission to perform the duties and carry out the objects for which it was created; and for the purposes of this act the Commission shall have power to require the attendance and testimony of witnesses and the production of all books, papers, tariffs, contracts, agreements, and documents relating to any matter under investigation, and to that end may invoke the aid of any court of the United States in requiring the attendance and testimony of witnesses and the production of books, papers, and documents under the provisions of this section.

Approved, February 4, 1887

[Endorsements]

Portions of transcription courtesy of Civics Online and Great Source Education Group.

5 The Sherman Antitrust Act, 1890

Fifty-first Congress of the United States of America, At the First Session,

Begun and held at the City of Washington on Monday, the second day of December, one thousand eight hundred and eighty-nine.

An act to protect trade and commerce against unlawful restraints and monopolies.

Be it enacted by the Senate and House of Representatives of the United States of America in Congress assembled,
Sec. 1. Every contract, combination in the form of trust or other- wise, or conspiracy, in restraint of trade or commerce among the several States, or with foreign nations, is hereby declared to be illegal. Every person who shall make any such contract or engage in any such combination or conspiracy, shall be deemed guilty of a misdemeanor, and, on conviction thereof, shall be punished by fine not exceeding five thousand dollars, or by imprisonment not exceeding one year, or by both said punishments, at the discretion of the court.

Sec. 2. Every person who shall monopolize, or attempt to monopolize, or combine or conspire with any other person or persons, to monopolize any part of the trade or commerce among the several States, or with foreign nations, shall be deemed guilty of a misdemeanor, and, on conviction thereof; shall be punished by fine not exceeding five thousand dollars, or by imprisonment not exceeding one year, or by both said punishments, in the discretion of the court.

Sec. 3. Every contract, combination in form of trust or otherwise, or conspiracy, in restraint of trade or commerce in any Territory of the United States or of the District of Columbia, or in restraint of trade or commerce between any such Territory and another, or between any such Territory or Territories and any State or States or the District of Columbia, or with foreign nations, or between the District of Columbia and any State or States or foreign nations, is hereby declared illegal. Every person who shall make any such contract or engage in any such combination or conspiracy, shall be deemed guilty of a misdemeanor, and, on conviction thereof, shall be punished by fine not exceeding five thousand dollars, or by imprisonment not exceeding one year, or by both said punishments, in the discretion of the court.

Sec. 4. The several circuit courts of the United States are hereby invested with jurisdiction to prevent and restrain violations of this act; and it shall be the duty of the several district attorneys of the United States, in their respective districts, under the direction of the Attorney-General, to institute proceedings in equity to prevent and restrain such violations. Such proceedings may be by way of petition setting forth the case and praying that such violation shall be enjoined or otherwise prohibited. When the parties complained of shall have been duly notified of such petition the court shall proceed, as soon as may be, to the hearing and determination of the case; and pending such petition and before final decree, the court may at any time make such temporary restraining order or prohibition as shall be deemed just in the premises.

Sec. 5. Whenever it shall appear to the court before which any proceeding under section four of this act may be pending, that the ends of justice require that other parties should be brought before the court, the court may cause them to be summoned, whether they reside in the district in which the court is held or not; and subpoenas to that end may be served in any district by the marshal thereof.

Sec. 6. Any property owned under any contract or by any combination, or pursuant to any conspiracy (and being the subject thereof) mentioned in section one of this act, and being in the course of transportation from one State to another, or to a foreign country, shall be- forfeited to the United States, and may be seized and condemned by like proceedings as those provided by law for the forfeiture, seizure, and condemnation of property imported into the United States contrary to law.

Sec. 7. Any person who shall be injured in his business or property by any other person or corporation by reason of anything forbidden or declared to be unlawful by this act, may sue therefor in any circuit court of the United States in the district in which the defendant resides or is found, without. respect to the amount in controversy, and shall recover three fold the damages by him sustained, and the costs of suit, including a reasonable attorney's fee.

Sec. 8. That the word "person," or "persons," wherever used in this act shall be deemed to include corporations and associations existing under or authorized by the laws of either the United States, the laws of any of the Territories, the laws of any State, or the laws of any foreign country.

Approved, July 2, 1890.

[Endorsements]

6 The 16th Amendment to the Constitution, 1913

Sixty-first Congress of the United States of America, At the First Session,

Begun and held at the City of Washington on Monday, the fifteenth day of March, one thousand nine hundred and nine.

JOINT RESOLUTION
Proposing an amendment to the Constitution of the United States.

Resolved by the Senate and House of Representatives of the United States of America in Congress assembled (two-thirds of each House concurring therein), That the following article is proposed as an amendment to the Constitution of the United States, which, when ratified by the legislature of three-fourths of the several States, shall be valid to all intents and purposes as a part of the Constitution:

"**ARTICLE XVI.** The Congress shall have power to lay and collect taxes on incomes, from whatever source derived, without apportionment among the several States, and without regard to any census or enumeration."

[Endorsements]

7 The 17th Amendment to the Constitution, 1913

Sixty-second Congress of the United States of America; At the Second Session,

Begun and held at the City of Washington on Monday, the fourth day of December, one thousand nine hundred and eleven.

JOINT RESOLUTION
Proposing an amendment to the Constitution providing that Senators shall be elected by the people of the several States.

Resolved by the Senate and House of Representatives of the United States of America in Congress assembled (two-thirds of each House concurring therein), That in lieu of the first paragraph of section three of Article I of the Constitution of the United States, and in lieu of so much of paragraph two of the same section as relates to the filling of vacancies, the following be proposed as an amendment to the Constitution, which shall be valid to all intents and purposes as part of the Constitution when ratified by the legislatures of three-fourths of the States:

"The Senate of the United States shall be composed of two Senators from each State, elected by the people thereof, for six years; and each Senator shall have one vote. The electors in each State shall have the qualifications requisite for electors of the most numerous branch of the State legislatures.

"When vacancies happen in the representation of any State in the Senate, the executive authority of such State shall issue writs of election to fill such vacancies: *Provided,* That the legislature of any State may empower the executive thereof to make temporary appointments until the people fill the vacancies by election as the legislature may direct.

"This amendment shall not be so construed as to affect the election or term of any Senator chosen before it becomes valid as part of the Constitution."

8 The Keating-Owen Child Labor Act, 1916

Sixty-fourth Congress of the United States of America; At the First Session,

Begun and held at the City of Washington on Monday, the sixth day of December, one thousand nine hundred and fifteen.

AN ACT To prevent interstate commerce in the products of child labor, and for other purposes.

Be it enacted by the Senate and House of Representatives of the United States of America in Congress assembled, That no producer, manufacturer, or dealer shall ship or deliver for shipment in interstate or foreign commerce, any article or commodity the product of any mine or quarry situated in the United States, in which within thirty days prior to the time of the removal of such product therefrom children under the age of sixteen years have been employed or permitted to work, or any article or commodity the product of any mill, cannery, workshop, factory, or manufacturing establishment, situated in the United States, in which within thirty days prior to the removal of such product therefrom children under the age of fourteen years have been employed or permitted to work, or children between the ages of fourteen years and sixteen years have been employed or permitted to work more than eight hours in any day, or more than six days in any week, or after the hour of seven o'clock postmeridian, or before the hour of six o'clock antemeridian: *Provided*, That a prosecution and conviction of a defendant for the shipment or delivery for shipment of any article or commodity under the conditions herein prohibited shall be a bar to any further prosecution against the same defendant for shipments or deliveries for shipment of any such article or commodity before the beginning of said prosecution.

SEC. 2. That the Attorney General, the Secretary of Commerce and the Secretary of Labor shall constitute a board to make and publish from time to time uniform rules and regulations for carrying out the provisions of this Act.

SEC. 3. That for the purpose of securing proper enforcement of this Act the Secretary of Labor, or any person duly authorized by him, shall have authority to enter and inspect at any time mines quarries, mills, canneries, workshops, factories, manufacturing establishments, and other places in which goods are produced or held for interstate commerce; and the Secretary of Labor shall have authority to employ such assistance for the purposes of this Act as may from time to time be authorized by appropriation or other law.

SEC. 4. That it shall be the duty of each district attorney to whom the Secretary of Labor shall report any violation of this Act, or to whom any State factory or mining or quarry inspector, commissioner of labor, State medical inspector or school-attendance officer, or any other person shall present satisfactory evidence of any such violation to cause appropriate proceedings to be commenced and prosecuted in the proper courts of the United States without delay for the enforcement of the penalties in such cases herein provided: *Provided,* That nothing in this Act shall be construed to apply to bona fide boys' and girls' canning clubs recognized by the Agricultural Department of the several States and of the United States.

SEC. 5. That any person who violates any of the provisions of section one of this Act, or who refuses or obstructs entry or inspection authorized by section three of this Act, shall for each offense prior to the first conviction of such person under the provisions of this Act, be punished by a fine of not more than $200, and shall for each offense subsequent to such conviction be punished by a fine of not more than $1,000, nor less than $100, or by imprisonment for not more than three months, or by both such fine and imprisonment, in the discretion of the court: *Provided,* That no dealer shall be prosecuted under the provisions of this Act for a shipment, delivery for shipment, or transportation who establishes a guaranty issued by the person by whom the goods shipped or delivered for shipment or transportation were manufactured or produced, resident in the United States, to the effect that such goods were produced or manufactured in a mine or quarry in which within thirty days prior to their removal therefrom no children under the age of sixteen years were employed or permitted to work, or in a mill, cannery, workshop, factory, or manufacturing establishment in which within thirty days prior to the removal of such goods therefrom no children under the ages of fourteen years were employed or permitted to work, nor children between the ages of fourteen years and sixteen years employed or permitted to work more than eight hours in any day or more than six days in any week or after the hour of seven o'clock postmeridian o before the hour of six o'clock antemeridian; and in such event, if the guaranty contains any false statement or a material fact the guarantor shall be amenable to prosecution and to the fine or imprisonment provided by this section for violation of the provisions of this Act. .Said guaranty, to afford the protection above provided, shall contain the name and address of the person giving the same: And provided further, That no producer, manufacturer, or dealer shall be prosecuted under this Act for the shipment, delivery for shipment, or transportation of a product of any mine, quarry , mill, cannery, workshop, factory, or manufacturing establishment, if the only employment therein within thirty days prior to the removal of such product therefrom, of a child under the age of sixteen years has been that of a child as to whom the producer, or manufacturer has in; good faith procured, at the time of employing such child, and has since in good faith relied upon and kept on file a certificate, issued in such form, under such conditions, any by such persons as may be prescribed by the board, showing the child to be of such an age that the shipment, delivery for shipment, or transportation was not prohibited by this Act. Any person who knowingly makes a false statement or presents false evidence in or in relation to any such certificate or application therefor shall be amenable to prosecution and to the fine or imprisonment provided by this section for violations of this Act. In any State designated by the board, an employment certificate or other similar paper as to the age of the child, issued under the laws of that State and not inconsistent with the provisions of this Act, shall have the same force and effect as a certificate herein provided for.

SEC. 6. That the word "person" as used in this Act shall be construed to include any individual or corporation or the members of any partnership or other unincorporated association. The term "ship or deliver for shipment in interstate or foreign commerce" as used in this Act means to transport or to ship or deliver for shipment from any State or Territory or the District of Columbia to or through any other State or Territory or the District of Columbia or to any foreign country; and in the case of a dealer means only to transport or to ship or deliver for shipment from the State, Territory or district of manufacture or production.

SEC. 7. That this Act shall take effect from and after one year from the date of its passage.

Approved, September 1, 1916.

9 The 19th Amendment to the Constitution, 1920

Sixty-sixth Congress of the United States of America; At the First Session,

Begun and held at the City of Washington on Monday, the nineteenth day of May, one thousand nine hundred and nineteen.

JOINT RESOLUTION

Proposing an amendment to the Constitution extending the right of suffrage to women.

Resolved by the Senate and House of Representatives of the United States of America in Congress assembled (two-thirds of each House concurring therein), That the following article is proposed as an amendment to the Constitution, which shall be valid to all intents and purposes as part of the Constitution when ratified by the legislature of three-fourths of the several States.

"ARTICLE ———.

"The right of citizens of the United States to vote shall not be denied or abridged by the United States or by any State on account of sex.

Congress shall have power to enforce this article by appropriate legislation."

10 Germany Suggests an Alliance: the Zimmerman Telegram, 1917

(*Decoded message text of the Zimmermann Telegram*)

FROM 2nd from London # 5747.

"We intend to begin on the first of February unrestricted submarine warfare. We shall endeavor in spite of this to keep the United States of America neutral. In the event of this not succeeding, we make Mexico a proposal or alliance on the following basis: make war together, make peace together, generous financial support and an understanding on our part that Mexico is to reconquer the lost territory in Texas, New Mexico, and Arizona. The settlement in detail is left to you. You will inform the President of the above most secretly as soon as the outbreak of war with the United States of America is certain and add the suggestion that he should, on his own initiative, invite Japan to immediate adherence and at the same time mediate between Japan and ourselves. Please call the President's attention to the fact that the ruthless employment of our submarines now offers the prospect of compelling England in a few months to make peace." Signed, ZIMMERMANN.

11 President Woodrow Wilson Considers the Post-war World: The Fourteen Points Speech to Congress, 1918

It will be our wish and purpose that the processes of peace, when they are begun, shall be absolutely open and that they shall involve and permit henceforth no secret understandings of any kind. The day of conquest and aggrandizement is gone by; so is also the day of secret covenants entered into in the interest of particular governments and likely at some unlooked-for moment to upset the peace of the world. It is this happy fact, now clear to the view of every public man whose thoughts do not still linger in an age that is dead and gone, which makes it possible for every nation whose purposes are consistent with justice and the peace of the world to avow nor or at any other time the objects it has in view.

We entered this war because violations of right had occurred which touched us to the quick and made the life of our own people impossible unless they were corrected and the world secure once for all against their recurrence. What we demand in this war, therefore, is nothing peculiar to ourselves. It is that the world be made fit and safe to live in; and particularly that it be made safe for every peace-loving nation which, like our own, wishes to live its own life, determine its own institutions, be assured of justice and fair dealing by the other peoples of the world as against force and selfish aggression. All the peoples of the world are in effect partners in this interest, and for our own part we see very clearly that unless justice be done to others it will not be done to us. The programme of the world's peace, therefore, is our programme; and that programme, the only possible programme, as we see it, is this:

I. Open covenants of peace, openly arrived at, after which there shall be no private international understandings of any kind but diplomacy shall proceed always frankly and in the public view.

II. Absolute freedom of navigation upon the seas, outside territorial waters, alike in peace and in war, except as the seas may be closed in whole or in part by international action for the enforcement of international covenants.

III. The removal, so far as possible, of all economic barriers and the establishment of an equality of trade conditions among all the nations consenting to the peace and associating themselves for its maintenance.

IV. Adequate guarantees given and taken that national armaments will be reduced to the lowest point consistent with domestic safety.

V. A free, open-minded, and absolutely impartial adjustment of all colonial claims, based upon a strict observance of the principle that in determining all such questions of sovereignty the interests of the populations concerned must have equal weight with the equitable claims of the government whose title is to be determined.

VI. The evacuation of all Russian territory and such a settlement of all questions affecting Russia as will secure the best and freest cooperation of the other nations of the world in obtaining for her an unhampered and unembarrassed opportunity for the independent determination of her own political development and national policy and assure her of a sincere welcome into the society of free nations under institutions of her own choosing; and, more than a welcome, assistance also of every kind that she may need and may herself desire. The treatment accorded Russia by her sister nations in the months to come will be the acid test of their good will, of their comprehension of her needs as distinguished from their own interests, and of their intelligent and unselfish sympathy.

VII. Belgium, the whole world will agree, must be evacuated and restored, without any attempt to limit the sovereignty which she enjoys in common with all other free nations. No other single act will serve as this will serve to restore confidence among the nations in the laws which they have themselves set and determined for the government of their relations with one another. Without this healing act the whole structure and validity of international law is forever impaired.

VIII. All French territory should be freed and the invaded portions restored, and the wrong done to France by Prussia in 1871 in the matter of Alsace-Lorraine, which has unsettled the peace of the world for nearly fifty years, should be righted, in order that peace may once more be made secure in the interest of all.

IX. A readjustment of the frontiers of Italy should be effected along clearly recognizable lines of nationality.

X. The peoples of Austria-Hungary, whose place among the nations we wish to see safeguarded and assured, should be accorded the freest opportunity to autonomous development.

XI. Rumania, Serbia, and Montenegro should be evacuated; occupied territories restored; Serbia accorded free and secure access to the sea; and the relations of the several Balkan states to one another determined by friendly counsel along historically established lines of allegiance and nationality; and international guarantees of the political and economic independence and territorial integrity of the several Balkan states should be entered into.

XII. The turkish portion of the present Ottoman Empire should be assured a secure sovereignty, but the other nationalities which are now under Turkish rule should be assured an undoubted security of life and an absolutely unmolested opportunity of autonomous development, and the Dardanelles should be permanently opened as a free passage to the ships and commerce of all nations under international guarantees.

XIII. An independent Polish state should be erected which should include the territories inhabited by indisputably Polish populations, which should be assured a free and secure access to the sea, and whose political and economic independence and territorial integrity should be guaranteed by international covenant.

XIV. A general association of nations must be formed under specific covenants for the purpose of affording mutual guarantees of political independence and territorial integrity to great and small states alike.

In regard to these essential rectifications of wrong and assertions of right we feel ourselves to be intimate partners of all the governments and peoples associated together against the Imperialists. We cannot be separated in interest or divided in purpose. We stand together until the end.

For such arrangements and covenants we are willing to fight and to continue to fight until they are achieved; but only because we wish the right to prevail and desire a just and stable peace such as can be secured only by removing the chief provocations to war, which this programme does remove. We have no jealousy of German greatness, and there is nothing in this programme that impairs it. We grudge her no achievement or distinction of learning or of pacific enterprise such as have made her record very bright and very enviable. We do not wish to injure her or to block in any way her legitimate influence or power. We do not wish to fight her either with arms or with hostile arrangements of trade if she is willing to associate herself with us and the other peace- loving nations of the world in covenants of justice and law and fair dealing. We wish her only to accept a place of equality among the peoples of the world,—the new world in which we now live,—instead of a place of mastery.

Transcription courtesy of the Avalon Project at Yale Law School.

SECTION 3

DOCUMENTS OF WAR:
THE UNITED STATES, WORLD WAR II,
AND THE EARLY COLD WAR,
1940s–1950s

1 President Franklin Roosevelt Asks for War: Address to Congress, 1941

Mr. Vice President, and Mr. Speaker, and Members of the Senate and House of Representatives:

Yesterday, December 7, 1941—a date which will live in infamy—the United States of America was suddenly and deliberately attacked by naval and air forces of the Empire of Japan.

The United States was at peace with that Nation and, at the solicitation of Japan, was still in conversation with its Government and its Emperor looking toward the maintenance of peace in the Pacific. Indeed, one hour after Japanese air squadrons had commenced bombing in the American Island of Oahu, the Japanese Ambassador to the United States and his colleague delivered to our Secretary of State a formal reply to a recent American message. And while this reply stated that it seemed useless to continue the existing diplomatic negotiations, it contained no threat or hint of war or of armed attack.

It will be recorded that the distance of Hawaii from Japan makes it obvious that the attack was deliberately planned many days or even weeks ago. During the intervening time the Japanese Government has deliberately sought to deceive the United States by false statements and expressions of hope for continued peace.

The attack yesterday on the Hawaiian Islands has caused severe damage to American naval and military forces. I regret to tell you that very many American lives have been lost. In addition American ships have been reported torpedoed on the high seas between San Francisco and Honolulu.

Yesterday the Japanese Government also launched an attack against Malaya.
Last night Japanese forces attacked Hong Kong.
Last night Japanese forces attacked Guam.
Last night Japanese forces attacked the Philippine Islands.
Last night the Japanese attacked Wake Island. And this morning the Japanese attacked Midway Island.

Japan has, therefore, undertaken a surprise offensive extending throughout the Pacific area. The facts of yesterday and today speak for themselves. The people of the United States have already formed their opinions and well understand the implications to the very life and safety of our Nation.

As Commander in Chief of the Army and Navy I have directed that all measures be taken for our defense.

But always will our whole Nation remember the character of the onslaught against us.

No matter how long it may take us to overcome this premeditated invasion, the American people in their righteous might will win through to absolute victory. I believe that I interpret the will of the Congress and of the people when I assert that we will not only defend ourselves to the uttermost but will make it very certain that this form of treachery shall never again endanger us.

Hostilities exist. There is no blinking at the fact that our people, our territory, and our interests are in grave danger.

With confidence in our armed forces—with the unbounding determination of our people—we will gain the inevitable triumph- so help us God.

I ask that the Congress declare that since the unprovoked and dastardly attack by Japan on Sunday, December 7, 1941, a state of war has existed between the United States and the Japanese Empire.

2 The Lend-Lease Act, 1941

A BILL
Further to promote the defense of the United States, and for other purposes.

Be it enacted by the Senate add House of Representatives of the United States of America in Congress assembled, That this Act may be cited as "An Act to Promote the Defense of the United States".

SEC. 2. As used in this Act -

(a) The term "defense article" means -

(1) Any weapon, munition. aircraft, vessel, or boat;

(2) Any machinery, facility, tool, material, or supply necessary for the manufacture, production, processing, repair, servicing, or operation of any article described in this subsection;

(3) Any component material or part of or equipment for any article described in this subsection;

(4) Any agricultural, industrial or other commodity or article for defense.

Such term "defense article" includes any article described in this subsection: Manufactured or procured pursuant to section 3, or to which the United States or any foreign government has or hereafter acquires title, possession, or control.

(b) The term "defense information" means any plan, specification, design, prototype, or information pertaining to any defense article.

SEC. 3. (a) Notwithstanding the provisions of any other law, the President may, from time to time. when he deems it in the interest of national defense, authorize the Secretary Of War, the Secretary of the Navy, or the bead of any other department or agency of the Government -

(1) To manufacture in arsenals, factories, and shipyards under their jurisdiction, or otherwise procure, to the extent to which funds are made available therefor, or contracts are authorized from time to time by the Congress, or both, any defense article for the government of any country whose defense the President deems vital to the defense of the United States.

(2) To sell, transfer title to, exchange, lease, lend, or otherwise dispose of, to any such government any defense article, but no defense article not manufactured or procured under paragraph (1) shall in any way be disposed of under this paragraph, except after consultation with the Chief of Staff of the Army or the Chief of Naval Operations of the Navy, or both. The value of defense articles disposed of in any way under authority of this paragraph, and procured from funds heretofore appropriated, shall not exceed $1,300,000,000. The value of such defense articles shall be determined by the head of the department or agency concerned or such other department, agency or officer as shall be designated in the manner provided in the rules and regulations issued hereunder. Defense articles procured from funds hereafter appropriated to any department or agency of the Government, other than from funds authorized to he appropriated under this Act. shall not be disposed of in any way under authority of this paragraph except to the extent hereafter authorized by the Congress in the Acts appropriating such funds or otherwise.

(3) To test, inspect, prove, repair, outfit, recondition, or otherwise to place in good working order, to the extent to which funds are made available therefor, or contracts are authorized from time to time by the Congress, or both, any defense article for any such government, or to procure any or all such services by private contract.

(4) To communicate to any such government any defense information pertaining to any defense article furnished to such government under paragraph (2) of this subsection.

(5) To release for export any defense article disposed of in any way under this subsection to any such government.

(b) The terms and conditions upon which any such foreign government receives any aid authorized under subsection (a) shall be those which the President deems satisfactory, and the benefit to the United States may be payment or repayment in kind or property, or any other direct or indirect benefit which the President deems satisfactory.

3 President Franklin Roosevelt Attacks Discrimination in the Defense Industry: Executive Order 8802, 1941

Reaffirming Policy Of Full Participation In The Defense Program By All Persons, Regardless Of Race, Creed, Color, Or National Origin, And Directing Certain Action In Furtherance Of Said Policy

June 25, 1941

WHEREAS it is the policy of the United States to encourage full participation in the national defense program by all citizens of the United States, regardless of race, creed, color, or national origin, in the firm belief that the democratic way of life within the Nation can be defended successfully only with the help and support of all groups within its borders; and

WHEREAS there is evidence that available and needed workers have been barred from employment in industries engaged in defense production solely because of considerations of race, creed, color, or national origin, to the detriment of workers' morale and of national unity:

NOW, THEREFORE, by virtue of the authority vested in me by the Constitution and the statutes, and as a prerequisite to the successful conduct of our national defense production effort, I do hereby reaffirm the policy of the United States that there shall be no discrimination in the employment of workers in defense industries or government because of race, creed, color, or national origin, and I do hereby declare that it is the duty of employers and of labor organizations, in furtherance of said policy and of this order, to provide for the full and equitable participation of all workers in defense industries, without discrimination because of race, creed, color, or national origin;

And it is hereby ordered as follows:

1. All departments and agencies of the Government of the United States concerned with vocational and training programs for defense production shall take special measures appropriate to assure that such programs are administered without discrimination because of race, creed, color, or national origin;

2. All contracting agencies of the Government of the United States shall include in all defense contracts hereafter negotiated by them a provision obligating the contractor not to discriminate against any worker because of race, creed, color, or national origin;

3. There is established in the Office of Production Management a Committee on Fair Employment Practice, which shall consist of a chairman and four other members to be appointed by the President. The Chairman and members of the Committee shall serve as such without compensation but shall be entitled to actual and necessary transportation, subsistence and other expenses incidental to performance of their duties. The Committee shall receive and investigate complaints of discrimination in violation of the provisions of this order and shall take appropriate steps to redress grievances which it finds to be valid. The Committee shall also recommend to the several departments and agencies of the Government of the United States and to the President all measures which may be deemed by it necessary or proper to effectuate the provisions of this order.

Franklin D. Roosevelt
The White House,
June 25, 1941.

4 President Franklin Roosevelt Orders the Relocation of Japanese Americans: Executive Order 9066, 1942

Executive Order No. 9066

The President

Executive Order

Authorizing the Secretary of War to Prescribe Military Areas

Whereas the successful prosecution of the war requires every possible protection against espionage and against sabotage to national-defense material, national-defense premises, and national-defense utilities as defined in Section 4, Act of April 20, 1918, 40 Stat. 533, as amended by the Act of November 30, 1940, 54 Stat. 1220, and the Act of August 21, 1941, 55 Stat. 655 (U.S.C., Title 50, Sec. 104);

Now, therefore, by virtue of the authority vested in me as President of the United States, and Commander in Chief of the Army and Navy, I hereby authorize and direct the Secretary of War, and the Military Commanders whom he may from time to time designate, whenever he or any designated Commander deems such action necessary or desirable, to prescribe military areas in such places and of such extent as he or the appropriate Military Commander may determine, from which any or all persons may be excluded, and with respect to which, the right of any person to enter, remain in, or leave shall be subject to whatever restrictions the Secretary of War or the appropriate Military Commander may impose in his discretion. The Secretary of War is hereby authorized to provide for residents of any such area who are excluded therefrom, such transportation, food, shelter, and other accommodations as may be necessary, in the judgment of the Secretary of War or the said Military Commander, and until other arrangements are made, to accomplish the purpose of this order. The designation of military areas in any region or locality shall supersede designations of prohibited and restricted areas by the Attorney General under the Proclamations of December 7 and 8, 1941, and shall supersede the responsibility and authority of the Attorney General under the said Proclamations in respect of such prohibited and restricted areas.

I hereby further authorize and direct the Secretary of War and the said Military Commanders to take such other steps as he or the appropriate Military Commander may deem advisable to enforce compliance with the restrictions applicable to each Military area hereinabove authorized to be designated, including the use of Federal troops and other Federal Agencies, with authority to accept assistance of state and local agencies.

I hereby further authorize and direct all Executive Departments, independent establishments and other Federal Agencies, to assist the Secretary of War or the said Military Commanders in carrying out this Executive Order, including the furnishing of medical aid, hospitalization, food, clothing, transportation, use of land, shelter, and other supplies, equipment, utilities, facilities, and services.

This order shall not be construed as modifying or limiting in any way the authority heretofore granted under Executive Order No. 8972, dated December 12, 1941, nor shall it be construed as limiting or modifying the duty and responsibility of the Federal Bureau of Investigation, with respect to the investigation of alleged acts of sabotage or the duty and responsibility of the Attorney General and the Department of Justice under the Proclamations of December 7 and 8, 1941, prescribing regulations for the conduct and control of alien enemies, except as such duty and responsibility is superseded by the designation of military areas hereunder.

Franklin D. Roosevelt

The White House,

February 19, 1942.

5 Initiating D-Day: General Dwight Eisenhower's Order of the Day, June 6, 1944

SUPREME HEADQUARTERS
ALLIED EXPEDITIONARY FORCE

Soldiers, Sailors, and Airmen of the Allied Expeditionary Force!

You are about to embark upon the Great Crusade, toward which we have striven these many months. The eyes of the world are upon you. The hope and prayers of liberty-loving people everywhere march with you. In company with our brave Allies and brothers-in-arms on other Fronts, you will bring about the destruction of the German war machine, the elimination of Nazi tyranny over the oppressed peoples of Europe, and security for ourselves in a free world.

Your task will not be an easy one. Your enemy is will trained, well equipped and battle-hardened. He will fight savagely.

But this is the year 1944! Much has happened since the Nazi triumphs of 1940-41. The United Nations have inflicted upon the Germans great defeats, in open battle, man-to-man. Our air offensive has seriously reduced their strength in the air and their capacity to wage war on the ground. Our Home Fronts have given us an overwhelming superiority in weapons and munitions of war, and placed at our disposal great reserves of trained fighting men. The tide has turned! The free men of the world are marching together to Victory!

I have full confidence in your courage, devotion to duty and skill in battle. We will accept nothing less than full Victory!

Good luck! And let us beseech the blessing of Almighty God upon this great and noble undertaking.

6 The Truman Doctrine, 1947

Mr. President, Mr. Speaker, Members of the Congress of the United States:

The gravity of the situation which confronts the world today necessitates my appearance before a joint session of the Congress. The foreign policy and the national security of this country are involved.

One aspect of the present situation, which I wish to present to you at this time for your consideration and decision, concerns Greece and Turkey.

The United States has received from the Greek Government an urgent appeal for financial and economic assistance. Preliminary reports from the American Economic Mission now in Greece and reports from the American Ambassador in Greece corroborate the statement of the Greek Government that assistance is imperative if Greece is to survive as a free nation.

I do not believe that the American people and the Congress wish to turn a deaf ear to the appeal of the Greek Government.

Greece is not a rich country. Lack of sufficient natural resources has always forced the Greek people to work hard to make both ends meet. Since 1940, this industrious and peace loving country has suffered invasion, four years of cruel enemy occupation, and bitter internal strife.

When forces of liberation entered Greece they found that the retreating Germans had destroyed virtually all the railways, roads, port facilities, communications, and merchant marine. More than a thousand villages had been burned. Eighty-five per cent of the children were tubercular. Livestock, poultry, and draft animals had almost disappeared. Inflation had wiped out practically all savings.

As a result of these tragic conditions, a militant minority, exploiting human want and misery, was able to create political chaos which, until now, has made economic recovery impossible.

Greece is today without funds to finance the importation of those goods which are essential to bare subsistence. Under these circumstances the people of Greece cannot make progress in solving their problems of reconstruction. Greece is in desperate need of financial and economic assistance to enable it to resume purchases of food, clothing, fuel and seeds. These are indispensable for the subsistence of its people and are obtainable only from abroad. Greece must have help to import the goods necessary to restore internal order and security, so essential for economic and political recovery.

The Greek Government has also asked for the assistance of experienced American administrators, economists and technicians to insure that the financial and other aid given to Greece shall be used effectively in creating a stable and self-sustaining economy and in improving its public administration.

The very existence of the Greek state is today threatened by the terrorist activities of several thousand armed men, led by Communists, who defy the government's authority at a number of points, particularly along the northern boundaries. A Commission appointed by the United Nations security Council is at present investigating disturbed conditions in northern Greece and alleged border violations along the frontier between Greece on the one hand and Albania, Bulgaria, and Yugoslavia on the other.

Meanwhile, the Greek Government is unable to cope with the situation. The Greek army is small and poorly equipped. It needs supplies and equipment if it is to restore the authority of the government throughout Greek territory. Greece must have assistance if it is to become a self-supporting and self-respecting democracy.

The United States must supply that assistance. We have already extended to Greece certain types of relief and economic aid but these are inadequate.

There is no other country to which democratic Greece can turn.

No other nation is willing and able to provide the necessary support for a democratic Greek government.

The British Government, which has been helping Greece, can give no further financial or economic aid after March 31. Great Britain finds itself under the necessity of reducing or liquidating its commitments in several parts of the world, including Greece.

We have considered how the United Nations might assist in this crisis. But the situation is an urgent one requiring immediate action and the United Nations and its related organizations are not in a position to extend help of the kind that is required.

It is important to note that the Greek Government has asked for our aid in utilizing effectively the financial and other assistance we may give to Greece, and in improving its public administration. It is of the utmost importance that we supervise the use of any funds made available to Greece; in such a manner that each dollar spent will count toward making Greece self-supporting, and will help to build an economy in which a healthy democracy can flourish.

No government is perfect. One of the chief virtues of a democracy, however, is that its defects are always visible and under democratic processes can be pointed out and corrected. The Government of Greece is not perfect. Nevertheless it represents eighty-five per cent of the members of the Greek Parliament who were chosen in an election last year. Foreign observers, including 692 Americans, considered this election to be a fair expression of the views of the Greek people.

The Greek Government has been operating in an atmosphere of chaos and extremism. It has made mistakes. The extension of aid by this country does not mean that the United States condones everything that the Greek Government has done or will do. We have condemned in the past, and we condemn now, extremist measures of the right or the left. We have in the past advised tolerance, and we advise tolerance now.

Greece's neighbor, Turkey, also deserves our attention.

The future of Turkey as an independent and economically sound state is clearly no less important to the freedom-loving peoples of the world than the future of Greece. The circumstances in which Turkey finds itself today are considerably different from those of Greece. Turkey has been spared the disasters that have beset Greece. And during the war, the United States and Great Britain furnished Turkey with material aid.

Nevertheless, Turkey now needs our support.

Since the war Turkey has sought financial assistance from Great Britain and the United States for the purpose of effecting that modernization necessary for the maintenance of its national integrity.

That integrity is essential to the preservation of order in the Middle East.

The British government has informed us that, owing to its own difficulties can no longer extend financial or economic aid to Turkey.

As in the case of Greece, if Turkey is to have the assistance it needs, the United States must supply it. We are the only country able to provide that help.

I am fully aware of the broad implications involved if the United States extends assistance to Greece and Turkey, and I shall discuss these implications with you at this time.

One of the primary objectives of the foreign policy of the United States is the creation of conditions in which we and other nations will be able to work out a way of life free from coercion. This was a fundamental issue in the war with Germany and Japan. Our victory was won over countries which sought to impose their will, and their way of life, upon other nations.

To ensure the peaceful development of nations, free from coercion, the United States has taken a leading part in establishing the United Nations, The United Nations is designed to make possible lasting freedom and independence for all its members. We shall not realize our objectives, however, unless we are willing to help free peoples to maintain their free institutions and their national integrity against aggressive movements that seek to impose upon them totalitarian regimes. This is no more than a frank recognition that totalitarian regimes imposed on free peoples, by direct or indirect aggression, undermine the foundations of international peace and hence the security of the United States.

The peoples of a number of countries of the world have recently had totalitarian regimes forced upon them against their will. The Government of the United States has made frequent protests against coercion and intimidation, in violation of the Yalta agreement, in Poland, Rumania, and Bulgaria. I must also state that in a number of other countries there have been similar developments.

At the present moment in world history nearly every nation must choose between alternative ways of life. The choice is too often not a free one.

One way of life is based upon the will of the majority, and is distinguished by free institutions, representative government, free elections, guarantees of individual liberty, freedom of speech and religion, and freedom from political oppression.

The second way of life is based upon the will of a minority forcibly imposed upon the majority. It relies upon terror and oppression, a controlled press and radio; fixed elections, and the suppression of personal freedoms.

I believe that it must be the policy of the United States to support free peoples who are resisting attempted subjugation by armed minorities or by outside pressures.

I believe that we must assist free peoples to work out their own destinies in their own way.

I believe that our help should be primarily through economic and financial aid which is essential to economic stability and orderly political processes.

Should we fail to aid Greece and Turkey in this fateful hour, the effect will be far reaching to the West as well as to the East.

We must take immediate and resolute action.

I therefore ask the Congress to provide authority for assistance to Greece and Turkey in the amount of $400,000,000 for the period ending June 30, 1948. In requesting these funds, I have taken into consideration the maximum amount of relief assistance which would be furnished to Greece out of the $350,000,000 which I recently requested that the Congress authorize for the prevention of starvation and suffering in countries devastated by the war.

In addition to funds, I ask the Congress to authorize the detail of American civilian and military personnel to Greece and Turkey, at the request of those countries, to assist in the tasks of reconstruction, and for the purpose of supervising the use of such financial and material assistance as may be furnished. I recommend that authority also be provided for the instruction and training of selected Greek and Turkish personnel.

Finally, I ask that the Congress provide authority which will permit the speediest and most effective use, in terms of needed commodities, supplies, and equipment, of such funds as may be authorized.

If further funds, or further authority, should be needed for purposes indicated in this message, I shall not hesitate to bring the situation before the Congress. On this subject the Executive and Legislative branches of the Government must work together.

This is a serious course upon which we embark.

The seeds of totalitarian regimes are nurtured by misery and want. They spread and grow in the evil soil of poverty and strife. They reach their full growth when the hope of a people for a better life has died. We must keep that hope alive.

The free peoples of the world look to us for support in maintaining their freedoms.

If we falter in our leadership, we may endanger the peace of the world—and we shall surely endanger the welfare of our own nation.

Great responsibilities have been placed upon us by the swift movement of events.

I am confident that the Congress will face these responsibilities squarely.

7 The Marshall Plan, 1948

THE MARSHALL PLAN (1948)

I need not tell you gentlemen that the world situation is very serious. That must be apparent to all intelligent people. I think one difficulty is that the problem is one of such enormous complexity that the very mass of facts presented to the public by press and radio make it exceedingly difficult for the man in the street to reach a clear appraisement of the situation. Furthermore, the people of this country are distant from the troubled areas of the earth and it is hard for them to comprehend the plight and consequent reaction of the long-suffering peoples, and the effect of those reactions on their governments in connection with our efforts to promote peace in the world.

In considering the requirements for the rehabilitation of Europe the physical loss of life, the visible destruction of cities, factories, mines, and railroads was correctly estimated, but it has become obvious during recent months that this visible destruction was probably less serious than the dislocation of the entire fabric of European economy. For the past 10 years conditions have been highly abnormal. The feverish maintenance of the war effort engulfed all aspects of national economics. Machinery has fallen into disrepair or is entirely obsolete. Under the arbitrary and destructive Nazi rule, virtually every possible enterprise was geared into the German war machine. Long-standing commercial ties, private institutions, banks, insurance companies and shipping companies disappeared, through the loss of capital, absorption through nationalization or by simple destruction. In many countries, confidence in the local currency has been severely shaken. The breakdown of the business structure of Europe during the war was complete. Recovery has been seriously retarded by the fact that 2 years after the close of hostilities a peace settlement with Germany and Austria has not been agreed upon. But even given a more prompt solution of these difficult problems, the rehabilitation of the economic structure of Europe quite evidently will require a much longer time and greater effort than had been foreseen.

There is a phase of this matter which is both interesting and serious. The farmer has always produced the foodstuffs to exchange with the city dweller for the other necessities of life. This division of labor is the basis of modern civilization. At the present time it is threatened with breakdown. The town and city industries are not producing adequate goods to exchange with the food-producing farmer. Raw materials and fuel are in short supply. Machinery is lacking or worn out. The farmer or the peasant cannot find the goods for sale which he desires to purchase. So the sale of his farm produce for money which he cannot use seems to him unprofitable transaction. He, therefore, has withdrawn many fields from crop cultivation and is using them for grazing. He feeds more grain to stock and finds for himself and his family an ample supply of food, however short he may be on clothing and the other ordinary gadgets of civilization. Meanwhile people in the cities are short of food and fuel. So the governments are forced to use their foreign money and credits to procure these necessities abroad. This process exhausts funds which are urgently needed for reconstruction. Thus a very serious situation is rapidly developing which bodes no good for the world. The modern system of the division of labor upon which the exchange of products is based is in danger of breaking down.

The truth of the matter is that Europe's requirements for the next 3 or 4 years of foreign food and other essential products—principally from America—are so much greater than her present ability to pay that she must have substantial additional help, or face economic, social, and political deterioration of a very grave character.

The remedy lies in breaking the vicious circle and restoring the confidence of the European people in the economic future of their own countries and of Europe as a whole. The manufacturer and the farmer throughout wide areas must be able and willing to exchange their products for currencies the continuing value of which is not open to question.

Aside from the demoralizing effect on the world at large and the possibilities of disturbances arising as a result of the desperation of the people concerned, the consequences to the economy of the United States should be apparent to all. It is logical that the United States should do whatever it is able to do to assist in the return of normal economic health in the world, without which there can be no political stability and no assured peace. Our policy is directed not against any country or doctrine but against hunger, poverty, desperation, and chaos. Its purpose should be the revival of working economy in the world so as to permit the emergence of political and social conditions in which free institutions can exist. Such assistance, I am convinced, must not be on a piecemeal basis as various crises develop. Any assistance that this Government may render in the future should provide a cure rather than a mere palliative. Any government that is willing to assist in the task of recovery will find full cooperation, I am sure, on the part of the United States Government. Any government which maneuvers to block the recovery of other countries cannot expect help from us. Furthermore, governments, political parties, or groups which seek to perpetuate human misery in order to profit therefrom politically or otherwise will encounter the opposition of the United States.

It is already evident that, before the United States Government can proceed much further in its efforts to alleviate the situation and help start the European world on its way to recovery, there must be some agreement among the countries of Europe as to the requirements of the situation and the part those countries themselves will take in order to give proper effect to whatever action might be undertaken by this Government. It would be neither fitting nor efficacious for this Government to undertake to draw up unilaterally a program designed to place Europe on its feet economically. This is the business of the Europeans. The initiative, I think, must come from Europe. The role of this country should consist of friendly aid in the drafting of a European program so far as it may be practical for us to do so. The program should be a joint one, agreed to by a number, if not all European nations.

An essential part of any successful action on the part of the United States is an understanding on the part of the people of America of the character of the problem and the remedies to be applied. Political passion and prejudice should have no part. With foresight, and a willingness on the part of our people to face up to the vast responsibilities which history has clearly placed upon our country, the difficulties I have outlined can and will be overcome.

8 President Harry Truman Orders the Desegregation of the Armed Forces: Executive Order 9981, 1948

Establishing the President's Committee on Equality of Treatment and Opportunity In the Armed Forces.

WHEREAS it is essential that there be maintained in the armed services of the United States the highest standards of democracy, with equality of treatment and opportunity for all those who serve in our country's defense:

NOW THEREFORE, by virtue of the authority vested in me as President of the United States, by the Constitution and the statutes of the United States, and as Commander in Chief of the armed services, it is hereby ordered as follows:

1. It is hereby declared to be the policy of the President that there shall be equality of treatment and opportunity for all persons in the armed services without regard to race, color, religion or national origin. This policy shall be put into effect as rapidly as possible, having due regard to the time required to effectuate any necessary changes without impairing efficiency or morale.

2. There shall be created in the National Military Establishment an advisory committee to be known as the President's Committee on Equality of Treatment and Opportunity in the Armed Services, which shall be composed of seven members to be designated by the President.

3. The Committee is authorized on behalf of the President to examine into the rules, procedures and practices of the Armed Services in order to determine in what respect such rules, procedures and practices may be altered or improved with a view to carrying out the policy of this order. The Committee shall confer and advise the Secretary of Defense, the Secretary of the Army, the Secretary of the Navy, and the Secretary of the Air Force, and shall make such recommendations to the President and to said Secretaries as in the judgment of the Committee will effectuate the policy hereof.

4. All executive departments and agencies of the Federal Government are authorized and directed to cooperate with the Committee in its work, and to furnish the Committee such information or the services of such persons as the Committee may require in the performance of its duties.

5. When requested by the Committee to do so, persons in the armed services or in any of the executive departments and agencies of the Federal Gov-

ernemt shall testify before the Committee and shall make available for use of the Committee such documents and other information as the Committee may require.

6. The Committee shall continue to exist until such time as the President shall terminate its existence by Executive order.

Harry Truman

The White House
July 26, 1948

Section 4

The Struggle for Equality and the Longest War, 1950s–1960s

1 "Hearts and Minds": Excerpt from the Supreme Court Ruling in the Case of *Brown v. Board of Education*, 1954

SUPREME COURT OF THE UNITED STATES

Brown v. Board of Education, 347 U.S. 483 (1954)(USSC+)

Argued December 9, 1952

Reargued December 8, 1953

Decided May 17, 1954

APPEAL FROM THE UNITED STATES DISTRICT COURT FOR THE DISTRICT OF KANSAS*

Opinion

MR. CHIEF JUSTICE WARREN delivered the opinion of the Court.

These cases come to us from the States of Kansas, South Carolina, Virginia, and Delaware. They are premised on different facts and different local conditions, but a common legal question justifies their consideration together in this consolidated opinion.

In each of the cases, minors of the Negro race, through their legal representatives, seek the aid of the courts in obtaining admission to the public schools of their community on a nonsegregated basis. In each instance, they had been denied admission to schools attended by white children under laws requiring or permitting segregation according to race. This segregation was alleged to deprive the plaintiffs of the equal protection of the laws under the Fourteenth Amendment. In each of the cases other than the Delaware case, a three-judge federal district court denied relief to the plaintiffs on the so-called "separate but equal" doctrine announced by this Court in Plessy v. Ferguson, 163 U.S. 537. Under that doctrine, equality of treatment is accorded when the races are provided substantially equal facilities, even though these facilities be separate. In the Delaware case, the Supreme Court of Delaware adhered to that doctrine, but ordered that the plaintiffs be admitted to the white schools because of their superiority to the Negro schools.

The plaintiffs contend that segregated public schools are not "equal" and cannot be made "equal," and that hence they are deprived of the equal protection of the laws. Because of the obvious importance of the question presented, the Court took jurisdiction. Argument was heard in the 1952 Term, and reargument was heard this Term on certain questions propounded by the Court.

Reargument was largely devoted to the circumstances surrounding the adoption of the Fourteenth Amendment in 1868. It covered exhaustively consideration of the Amendment in Congress, ratification by the states, then-existing practices in racial segregation, and the views of proponents and opponents of the Amendment. This discussion and our own investigation convince us that, although these sources cast some light, it is not enough to resolve the problem with which we are faced. At best, they are inconclusive. The most avid proponents of the post-War Amendments undoubtedly intended them to remove all legal distinctions among "all persons born or naturalized in the United States." Their opponents, just as certainly, were antagonistic to both the letter and the spirit of the Amendments and wished them to have the most limited effect. What others in Congress and the state legislatures had in mind cannot be determined with any degree of certainty.

An additional reason for the inconclusive nature of the Amendment's history with respect to segregated schools is the status of public education at that time. In the South, the movement toward free common schools, supported by general taxation, had not yet taken hold. Education of white children was largely in the hands of private groups. Education of Negroes was almost nonexistent, and practically all of the race were illiterate. In fact, any education of Negroes was forbidden by law in some states. Today, in contrast, many Negroes have achieved outstanding success in the arts and sciences, as well as in the business and professional world. It is true that public school education at the time of the Amendment had advanced further in the North, but the effect of the Amendment on Northern States was generally ignored in the congressional debates. Even in the North, the conditions of public education did not approximate those existing today. The curriculum was usually rudimentary; ungraded schools were common in rural areas; the school term was but three months a year in many states, and compulsory school attendance was virtually unknown. As a consequence, it is not surprising that there should be so little in the history of the Fourteenth Amendment relating to its intended effect on public education.

In the first cases in this Court construing the Fourteenth Amendment, decided shortly after its adoption, the Court interpreted it as proscribing all state-imposed discriminations against the Negro race. The doctrine of "separate but equal" did not make its appearance in this Court until 1896 in the case of *Plessy v. Ferguson*, supra, involving not education but transportation. American courts have since labored with the doctrine for over half a century. In this Court, there have been six cases involving the "separate but equal" doctrine in the field of public education. In *Cumming v. County Board of Education*, 175 U.S. 528, and *Gong Lum v. Rice*, 275 U.S. 78, the validity of the doctrine itself was not challenged. In more recent cases, all on the graduate school level, inequality was found in that specific benefits enjoyed by white students were denied to Negro students of the same educational qualifications. Missouri ex rel. *Gaines v. Canada*, 305 U.S. 337; *Sipuel v. Oklahoma*, 332 U.S. 631; *Sweatt v. Painter*, 339 U.S. 629; *McLaurin v. Oklahoma State Regents*, 339 U.S. 637. In none of these cases was it necessary to reexamine the doctrine to grant relief to the Negro plaintiff. And in *Sweatt v. Painter*, supra, the Court expressly reserved decision on the question whether *Plessy v. Ferguson* should be held inapplicable to public education.

In the instant cases, that question is directly presented. Here, unlike *Sweatt v. Painter*, there are findings below that the Negro and white schools involved have been equalized, or are being equalized, with respect to buildings, curricula, qualifications and salaries of teachers, and other "tangible" factors. Our decision, therefore, cannot turn on merely a comparison of these tangible factors in the Negro and white schools involved in each of the cases. We must look instead to the effect of segregation itself on public education.

In approaching this problem, we cannot turn the clock back to 1868, when the Amendment was adopted, or even to 1896, when *Plessy v. Ferguson* was written. We must consider public education in the light of its full development and its present place in American life throughout the Nation. Only in this way can it be determined if segregation in public schools deprives these plaintiffs of the equal protection of the laws.

Today, education is perhaps the most important function of state and local governments. Compulsory school attendance laws and the great expenditures for education both demonstrate our recognition of the importance of education to our democratic society. It is required in the performance of our most basic public responsibilities, even service in the armed forces. It is the very foundation of good citizenship. Today it is a principal instrument in awakening the child to cultural values, in preparing him for later professional training, and in helping him to adjust normally to his environment. In these days, it is doubtful that any child may reasonably be expected to succeed in life if he is denied the opportunity of an education. Such an opportunity, where the state has undertaken to provide it, is a right which must be made available to all on equal terms.

We come then to the question presented: Does segregation of children in public schools solely on the basis of race, even though the physical facilities and other "tangible" factors may be equal, deprive the children of the minority group of equal educational opportunities? We believe that it does.

In *Sweatt v. Painter*, supra, in finding that a segregated law school for Negroes could not provide them equal educational opportunities, this Court relied in large part on "those qualities which are incapable of objective measurement but which make for greatness in a law school." In *McLaurin v. Oklahoma State Regents*, supra, the Court, in requiring that a Negro admitted to a white graduate school be treated like all other students, again resorted to intangible considerations: ". . . his ability to study, to engage in discussions and exchange views with other students, and, in general, to learn his profession." Such considerations apply with added force to children in grade and high schools. To separate them from others of similar age and qualifications solely because of their race generates a feeling of inferiority as to their status in the community that may affect their hearts and minds in a way unlikely ever to be undone. The effect of this separation on their educational opportunities was well stated by a finding in the Kansas case by a court which nevertheless felt compelled to rule against the Negro plaintiffs:

Segregation of white and colored children in public schools has a detrimental effect upon the colored children. The impact is greater when it has the sanction of the law, for the policy of separating the races is usually interpreted as denoting the inferiority of the negro group. A sense of inferiority affects the motivation of a child to learn. Segregation with the sanction of law, therefore, has a tendency to [retard] the educational and mental development of negro children and to deprive them of some of the benefits they would receive in a racial[ly] integrated school system.

Whatever may have been the extent of psychological knowledge at the time of *Plessy v. Ferguson*, this finding is amply supported by modern authority. Any language in *Plessy v. Ferguson* contrary to this finding is rejected.

We conclude that, in the field of public education, the doctrine of "separate but equal" has no place. Separate educational facilities are inherently unequal. Therefore, we hold that the plaintiffs and others similarly situated for whom the actions have been brought are, by reason of the segregation complained of, deprived of the equal protection of the laws guaranteed by the Fourteenth Amendment. This disposition makes unnecessary any discussion whether such segregation also violates the Due Process Clause of the Fourteenth Amendment.

2 Excerpt from the Civil Rights Act, 1964

An Act

To enforce the constitutional right to vote, to confer jurisdiction upon the district courts of the United States to provide injunctive relief against discrimination in public accommodations, to authorize the Attorney General to institute suits to protect constitutional rights in public facilities and public education, to extend the Commission on Civil Rights, to prevent discrimination in federally assisted programs, to establish a Commission on Equal Employment Opportunity, and for other purposes.

Be it enacted by the Senate and House of Representatives of the United States of America in Congress assembled, That this Act may be cited as the "Civil Rights Act of 1964".

TITLE I—VOTING RIGHTS
SEC. 101. Section 2004 of the Revised Statutes (42 U.S.C. 1971), as amended by section 131 of the Civil Rights Act of 1957 (71 Stat. 637), and as further amended by section 601 of the Civil Rights Act of 1960 (74 Stat. 90), is further amended as follows:

"(2) No person acting under color of law shall—

"(A) in determining whether any individual is qualified under State law or laws to vote in any Federal election, apply any standard, practice, or procedure different from the standards, practices, or procedures applied under such law or laws to other individuals within the same county, parish, or similar political subdivision who have been found by State officials to be qualified to vote;

"(B) deny the right of any individual to vote in any Federal election because of an error or omission on any record or paper relating to any application, registration, or other act requisite to voting, if such error or omission is not material in determining whether such individual is qualified under State law to vote in such election; or

"(C) employ any literacy test as a qualification for voting in any Federal election unless (i) such test is administered to each individual and is conducted wholly in writing, and (ii) a certified copy of the test and of the answers given by the individual is furnished to him within twenty-five days of the submission of his request made within the period of time during which records and papers are required to be retained and preserved pursuant to title III of the Civil Rights Act of 1960 (42 U.S.C. 1974—74e; 74 Stat. 88): Provided, however, That the Attorney General may enter into agreements with appropriate State or local authorities that preparation, conduct, and maintenance of such tests in accordance with the provisions of applicable State or local law, including such special provisions as are necessary in the preparation, conduct, and maintenance of such tests for persons who are blind or otherwise physically handicapped, meet the purposes of this subparagraph and constitute compliance therewith.

TITLE II—INJUNCTIVE RELIEF AGAINST DISCRIMINATION IN PLACES OF PUBLIC ACCOMMODATION

SEC. 201. (a) All persons shall be entitled to the full and equal enjoyment of the goods, services, facilities, and privileges, advantages, and accommodations of any place of public accommodation, as defined in this section, without discrimination or segregation on the ground of race, color, religion, or national origin.

(b) Each of the following establishments which serves the public is a place of public accommodation within the meaning of this title if its operations affect commerce, or if discrimination or segregation by it is supported by State action:

(1) any inn, hotel, motel, or other establishment which provides lodging to transient guests, other than an establishment located within a building which contains not more than five rooms for rent or hire and which is actually occupied by the proprietor of such establishment as his residence;

(2) any restaurant, cafeteria, lunchroom, lunch counter, soda fountain, or other facility principally engaged in selling food for consumption on the premises, including, but not limited to, any such facility located on the premises of any retail establishment; or any gasoline station;

(3) any motion picture house, theater, concert hall, sports arena, stadium or other place of exhibition or entertainment; and

(4) any establishment (A)(i) which is physically located within the premises of any establishment otherwise covered by this subsection, or (ii) within the premises of which is physically located any such covered establishment, and (B) which holds itself out as serving patrons of such covered establishment.

SEC. 202. All persons shall be entitled to be free, at any establishment or place, from discrimination or segregation of any kind on the ground of race, color, religion, or national origin, if such discrimination or segregation is or purports to be required by any law, statute, ordinance, regulation, rule, or order of a State or any agency or political subdivision thereof.

SEC. 203. No person shall (a) withhold, deny, or attempt to withhold or deny, or deprive or attempt to deprive, any person of any right or privilege secured by section 201 or 202, or (b) intimidate, threaten, or coerce, or attempt to intimidate, threaten, or coerce any person with the purpose of interfering with any right or privilege secured by section 201 or 202, or (c) punish or attempt to punish any person for exercising or attempting to exercise any right or privilege secured by section 201 or 202.

SEC. 204. (a) Whenever any person has engaged or there are reasonable grounds to believe that any person is about to engage in any act or practice prohibited by section 203, a civil action for preventive relief, including an application for a permanent or temporary injunction, restraining order, or other order, may be instituted by the person aggrieved and, upon timely application, the court may, in its discretion, permit the Attorney General to intervene in such civil action if he certifies that the case is of general public importance. Upon application by the complainant and in such circumstances as the court may deem just, the court may appoint an attorney for such complainant and may authorize the commencement of the civil action without the payment of fees, costs, or security.

SEC. 206. (a) Whenever the Attorney General has reasonable cause to believe that any person or group of persons is engaged in a pattern or practice of resistance to the full enjoyment of any of the rights secured by this title, and that the pattern or practice is of such a nature and is intended to deny the full exercise of the rights herein described, the Attorney General may bring a civil action in the appropriate district court of the United States by filing with it a complaint (1) signed by him (or in his absence the Acting Attorney General), (2) setting forth facts pertaining to such pattern or practice, and (3) requesting such preventive relief, including an application for a permanent or temporary injunction, restraining order or other order against the person or persons responsible for such pattern or practice, as he deems necessary to insure the full enjoyment of the rights herein described.

(b) In any such proceeding the Attorney General may file with the clerk of such court a request that a court of three judges be convened to hear and determine the case. Such request by the Attorney General shall be accompanied by a certificate that, in his opinion, the case is of general public importance. A copy of the certificate and request for a three-judge court shall be immediately furnished by such clerk to the chief judge of the circuit (or in his absence, the presiding circuit judge of the circuit) in which the case is pending. Upon receipt of the copy of such request it shall be the duty of the chief judge of the circuit or the presiding circuit judge, as the case may be, to designate immediately three judges in such circuit, of whom at least one shall be a circuit judge and another of whom shall be a district judge of the court in which the proceeding was instituted, to hear and determine such case, and it shall be the duty of the judges so designated to assign the case for hearing at the earliest practicable date, to participate in the hearing and determination thereof, and to cause the case to be in every way expedited. An appeal from the final judgment of such court will lie to the Supreme Court.

In the event the Attorney General fails to file such a request in any such proceeding, it shall be the duty of the chief judge of the district (or in his absence, the acting chief judge) in which the case is pending immediately to designate a judge in such district to hear and determine the case. In the event that no judge in the district is available to hear and determine the case, the chief judge of the district, or the acting chief judge, as the case may be, shall certify this fact to the chief judge of the circuit (or in his absence, the acting chief judge) who shall then designate a district or circuit judge of the circuit to hear and determine the case.

It shall be the duty of the judge designated pursuant to this section to assign the case for hearing at the earliest practicable date and to cause the case to be in every way expedited.

SEC. 207. (a) The district courts of the United States shall have jurisdiction of proceedings instituted pursuant to this title and shall exercise the same without regard to whether the aggrieved party shall have exhausted any administrative or other remedies that may be provided by law.

(b) The remedies provided in this title shall be the exclusive means of enforcing the rights based on this title, but nothing in this title shall preclude any individual or any State or local agency from asserting any right based on any other Federal or State law not inconsistent with this title, including any statute or ordinance requiring nondiscrimination in public establishments or accommodations, or from pursuing any remedy, civil or criminal, which may be available for the vindication or enforcement of such right.

TITLE III—DESEGREGATION OF PUBLIC FACILITIES

SEC. 301. (a) Whenever the Attorney General receives a complaint in writing signed by an individual to the effect that he is being deprived of or threatened with the loss of his right to the equal protection of the laws, on account of his race, color, religion, or national origin, by being denied equal utilization of any public facility which is owned, operated, or managed by or on behalf of any State or subdivision thereof, other than a public school or public college as defined in section 401 of title IV hereof, and the Attorney General believes the complaint is meritorious and certifies that the signer or signers of such complaint are unable, in his judgment, to initiate and maintain appropriate legal proceedings for relief and that the institution of an action will materially further the orderly progress of desegregation in public facilities, the Attorney General is authorized to institute for or in the name of the United States a civil action in any appropriate district court of the United States against such parties and for such relief as may be appropriate, and such court shall have and shall exercise jurisdiction of proceedings instituted pursuant to this section. The Attorney General may implead as defendants such additional parties as are or become necessary to the grant of effective relief hereunder.

"DUTIES OF THE COMMISSION
"SEC. 104. (a) The Commission shall—

"(1) investigate allegations in writing under oath or affirmation that certain citizens of the United States are being deprived of their right to vote and have that vote counted by reason of their color, race, religion, or national origin; which writing, under oath or affirmation, shall set forth the facts upon which such belief or beliefs are based;

"(2) study and collect information concerning legal developments constituting a denial of equal protection of the laws under the Constitution because of race, color, religion or national origin or in the administration of justice;

"(3) appraise the laws and policies of the Federal Government with respect to denials of equal protection of the laws under the Constitution because of race, color, religion or national origin or in the administration of justice;

"(4) serve as a national clearinghouse for information in respect to denials of equal protection of the laws because of race, color, religion or national origin, including but not limited to the fields of voting, education, housing, employment, the use of public facilities, and transportation, or in the administration of justice;

"(5) investigate allegations, made in writing and under oath or affirmation, that citizens of the United States are unlawfully being accorded or denied the right to vote, or to have their votes properly counted, in any election of presidential electors, Members of the United States Senate, or of the House of Representatives, as a result of any patterns or practice of fraud or discrimination in the conduct of such election; and

TITLE VI—NONDISCRIMINATION IN FEDERALLY ASSISTED PROGRAMS
SEC. 601. No person in the United States shall, on the ground of race, color, or national origin, be excluded from participation in, be denied the benefits of, or be subjected to discrimination under any program or activity receiving Federal financial assistance.

SEC. 602. Each Federal department and agency which is empowered to extend Federal financial assistance to any program or activity, by way of grant, loan, or contract other than a contract of insurance or guaranty, is authorized and directed to effectuate the provisions of section 601 with respect to such program or activity by issuing rules, regulations, or orders of general applicability which shall be consistent with achievement of the objectives of the statute authorizing the financial assistance in connection with which the action is taken. No such rule, regulation, or order shall become effective unless and until approved by the President. Compliance with any requirement adopted pursuant to this section may be effected (1) by the termination of or refusal to grant or to continue assistance under such program or activity to any recipient as to whom there has been an express finding on the record, after opportunity for hearing, of a failure to comply with such requirement, but such termination or refusal shall be limited to the particular political entity, or part thereof, or other recipient as to whom such a finding has been made and, shall be limited in its effect to the particular program, or part thereof, in which such noncompliance has been so found, or (2) by any other means authorized by law: Provided, however, That no such action shall be taken until the department or agency concerned has advised the appropriate person or persons of the failure to comply with the requirement and has determined that compliance cannot be secured by voluntary means. In the case of any action terminating, or refusing to grant or continue, assistance because of failure to comply with a requirement imposed pursuant to this section, the head of the federal department or agency shall file with the committees of the House and Senate having legislative jurisdiction over the program or activity involved a full written report of the circumstances and the grounds for such action. No such action shall become effective until thirty days have elapsed after the filing of such report.

SEC. 603. Any department or agency action taken pursuant to section 602 shall be subject to such judicial review as may otherwise be provided by law for similar action taken by such department or agency on other grounds. In the case of action, not otherwise subject to judicial review, terminating or refusing to grant or to continue financial assistance upon a finding of failure to comply with any requirement imposed pursuant to section 602, any person aggrieved (including any State or political subdivision thereof and any agency of either) may obtain judicial review of such action in accordance with section 10 of the Administrative Procedure Act, and such action shall not be deemed committed to unreviewable agency discretion within the meaning of that section.

TITLE VII—EQUAL EMPLOYMENT OPPORTUNITY
DEFINITIONS
SEC. 701. For the purposes of this title—

DISCRIMINATION BECAUSE OF RACE, COLOR, RELIGION, SEX, OR NATIONAL ORIGIN
SEC. 703. (a) It shall be an unlawful employment practice for an employer—

(1) to fail or refuse to hire or to discharge any individual, or otherwise to discriminate against any individual with respect to his compensation, terms,

conditions, or privileges of employment, because of such individual's race, color, religion, sex, or national origin; or

(2) to limit, segregate, or classify his employees in any way which would deprive or tend to deprive any individual of employment opportunities or otherwise adversely affect his status as an employee, because of such individual's race, color, religion, sex, or national origin.

(b) It shall be an unlawful employment practice for an employment agency to fail or refuse to refer for employment, or otherwise to discriminate against, any individual because of his race, color, religion, sex, or national origin, or to classify or refer for employment any individual on the basis of his race, color, religion, sex, or national origin.

(c) It shall be an unlawful employment practice for a labor organization—

(1) to exclude or to expel from its membership, or otherwise to discriminate against, any individual because of his race, color, religion, sex, or national origin;

(2) to limit, segregate, or classify its membership, or to classify or fail or refuse to refer for employment any individual, in any way which would deprive or tend to deprive any individual of employment opportunities, or would limit such employment opportunities or otherwise adversely affect his status as an employee or as an applicant for employment, because of such individual's race, color, religion, sex, or national origin; or

(3) to cause or attempt to cause an employer to discriminate against an individual in violation of this section.

(d) It shall be an unlawful employment practice for any employer, labor organization, or joint labor-management committee controlling apprenticeship or other training or retraining, including on-the-job training programs to discriminate against any individual because of his race, color, religion, sex, or national origin in admission to, or employment in, any program established to provide apprenticeship or other training.

OTHER UNLAWFUL EMPLOYMENT PRACTICES

SEC. 704. (a) It shall be an unlawful employment practice for an employer to discriminate against any of his employees or applicants for employment, for an employment agency to discriminate against any individual, or for a labor organization to discriminate against any member thereof or applicant for membership, because he has opposed, any practice made an unlawful employment practice by this title, or because he has made a charge, testified, assisted, or participated in any manner in an investigation, proceeding, or hearing under this title.

(b) It shall be an unlawful employment practice for an employer, labor organization, or employment agency to print or publish or cause to be printed or published any notice or advertisement relating to employment by such an employer or membership in or any classification or referral for employment by such a labor organization, or relating to any classification or referral for employment by such an employment agency, indicating any preference, limitation, specification, or discrimination, based on race, color, religion, sex, or national origin, except that such a notice or advertisement may indicate a preference, limitation, specification, or discrimination based on religion, sex, or national origin when religion, sex, or national origin is a bona fide occupational qualification for employment.

EQUAL EMPLOYMENT OPPORTUNITY COMMISSION
SEC. 705. (a) There is hereby created a Commission to be known as the Equal Employment Opportunity Commission, which shall be composed of five members, not more than three of whom shall be members of the same political party, who shall be appointed by the President by and with the advice and consent of the Senate. One of the original members shall be appointed for a term of one year, one for a term of two years, one for a term of three years, one for a term of four years, and one for a term of five years, beginning from the date of enactment of this title, but their successors shall be appointed for terms of five years each, except that any individual chosen to fill a vacancy shall be appointed only for the unexpired term of the member whom he shall succeed. The President shall designate one member to serve as Chairman of the Commission, and one member to serve as Vice Chairman. The Chairman shall be responsible on behalf of the Commission for the administrative operations of the Commission, and shall appoint, in accordance with the civil service laws, such officers, agents, attorneys, and employees as it deems necessary to assist it in the performance of its functions and to fix their compensation in accordance with the Classification Act of 1949, as amended. The Vice Chairman shall act as Chairman in the absence or disability of the Chairman or in the event of a vacancy in that office.

3 "The Possible Consequences of the Loss Are Just Incalculable": President Dwight Eisenhower Discusses the "Domino Theory," 1954

In a press conference on 7 April 1954, President Dwight D. Eisenhower articulates the domino thesis.

Q. ROBERT RICHARDS, COPLEY PRESS: Mr. President, would you mind commenting on the strategic importance of Indochina to the free world? I think there has been, across the country, some lack of understanding on just what it means to us.

THE PRESIDENT: You have, of course, both the specific and the general when you talk about such things.

First of all, you have the specific value of a locality in its production of materials that the world needs.

Then you have the possibility that many human beings pass under a dictatorship that is inimical to the free world.

Finally, you have broader considerations that might follow what you would call the 'falling domino' principle. You have a row of dominoes set up, you knock over the first one, and what will happen to the last one is the certainty that it will go over very quickly so you could have a beginning of a disintegration that would have the most profound influences.

Now, with respect to the first one, two of the items from this particular area that the world uses are tin and tungsten. They are very important. There are others, of course, the rubber plantations and so on.

Then with respect to more people passing under this domination, Asia, after all, has already lost some 450 million of its peoples to the Communist dictatorship, and we simply can't afford greater losses.

But when we come to the possible sequence of events, the loss of Indochina, of Burma, of Thailand, of the Peninsula, and Indonesia following, now you begin to talk about areas that not only multiply the disadvantages that you would suffer through loss of materials, sources of materials, but now you are talking really about millions and millions and millions of people.

Finally, the geographical position achieved thereby does many things. It turns the so-called island defensive chain of Japan, Formosa, of the Philippines and to the southward; it moves in to threaten Australia and New Zealand.

It takes away, in its economic aspects, that region that Japan must have as a trading area or Japan, in turn, will have only one place in the world to go—that is, toward the Communist areas in order to live.

So, the possible consequences of the loss are just incalculable to the free world.

4 "More Advantages Than . . . Risks": The Taylor Report, 1961

Cable by General Maxwell Taylor, Kennedy's military adviser, to the president, 1 November 1961, in which Taylor recommends the dispatch of US military force into South Vietnam.

This message is for the purpose of presenting my reasons for recommending the introduction of a U.S. military force into SVN [South Vietnam]. I have reached the conclusion that this is an essential action if we are to reverse the present downward trend of events in spite of a full recognition of the following disadvantages:

a. The strategic reserve of U.S. forces is presently so weak that we can ill afford any detachment of forces to a peripheral area of the Communist bloc where they will be pinned down for an uncertain duration.

b. Although U.S. prestige is already engaged in SVN, it will become more so by the sending of troops.

c. If the first contingent is not enough to accomplish the necessary results, it will be difficult to resist the pressure to reinforce. If the ultimate result sought is the closing of the frontiers and the clean-up of the insurgents within SVN, there is no limit to our possible commitment (unless we attack the source in Hanoi).

d. The introduction of U.S. forces may increase tensions and risk escalation into a major war in Asia.

On the other side of the argument, there can be no action so convincing of U.S. seriousness of purpose and hence so reassuring to the people and Government of SVN and to our other friends and allies in SEA [Southeast Asia] as the introduction of U.S. forces into SVN. The views of indigenous and U.S. officials consulted on our trip were unanimous on this point. I have just seen Saigon [cable] 575 to State and suggest that it be read in connection with this message.

The size of the U.S. force introduced need not be great to provide the military presence necessary to produce the desired effect on national morale in SVN and on international opinion. A bare token, however, will not suffice; it must have a significant value. The kinds of tasks which it might undertake which would have a significant value are suggested in Baguio [cable] 0005. They are:

a. Provide a U.S. military presence capable of raising national morale and of showing to SEA the seriousness of the U.S. intent to resist a Communist takeover.

b. Conduct logistical operations in support of military and flood relief operations.

c. Conduct such combat operations as are necessary for self-defense and for the security of the area in which they are stationed.

d. Provide an emergency reserve to back up the Armed Forces of the GVN in the case of a heightened military crisis.

e. Act as an advance party of such additional forces as may be introduced if CINCPAC [U.S. Commander in Chief, Pacific] or SEATO contingency plans are invoked.

It is noteworthy that this force is not proposed to clear the jungles and forests of VC [Vietcong] guerrillas. That should be the primary task of the Armed Forces of Vietnam for which they should be specifically organized, trained and stiffened with ample U.S. advisors down to combat battalion levels. However, the U.S. troops may be called upon to engage in combat to protect themselves, their working parties, and the area in which they live. As a general reserve, they might be thrown into action (with U.S. agreement) against large, formed guerrilla bands which have abandoned the forests for attacks on major targets. But in general, our forces should not engage in small-scale guerrilla operations in the jungle.

As an area for the operations of U.S. troops, SVN is not an excessively difficult or unpleasant place to operate. While the border areas are rugged and heavily forested, the terrain is comparable to parts of Korea where U.S. troops learned to live and work without too much effort. However, these border areas, for reasons stated above, are not the places to engage our forces. In the High Plateau and in the coastal plain where U.S. troops would probably be stationed, these jungle-forest conditions do not exist to any great extent. The most unpleasant feature in the coastal areas would be the heat and, in the Delta, the mud left behind by the flood. The High Plateau offers no particular obstacle to the stationing of U.S. troops.

The extent to which the Task Force would engage in flood relief activities in the Delta will depend upon further study of the problem there. As reported in Saigon 537, I see considerable advantages in playing up this aspect of the TF [Task Force] mission. I am presently inclined to favor a dual mission, initially help to the flood area and subsequently use in any other area of SVN where its resources can be used effectively to give tangible support in the struggle against the VC. However, the possibility of emphasizing the humanitarian mission will wane if we wait long in moving in our forces or in linking our stated purpose with the emergency conditions created by the flood.

The risks of backing into a major Asian war by way of SVN are present but are not impressive. NVN [North Vietnam] is extremely vulnerable to conventional bombing, a weakness which should be exploited diplomatically in convincing Hanoi to lay off SVN. Both the D.R.V. and the Chicoms [Chinese communists] would face severe logistical difficulties in trying to maintain strong forces in the field in SEA, difficulties which we share but by no means to the same degree. There is no case for fearing a mass onslaught of Communist manpower into SVN and its neighboring states, particularly if our airpower is allowed a free hand against logistical targets. Finally, the starvation conditions in China should discourage Communist leaders there from being militarily venturesome for some time to come.

By the foregoing line of reasoning, I have reached the conclusion that the introduction of [word illegible] military Task Force without delay offers definitely more advantage that it creates risks and difficulties. In fact, I do not believe that our program to save SVN will succeed without it. If the concept is approved, the exact size and composition of the force should be determined by Sec Def in consultation with the JCS, the Chief MAAG [Military Assistance Advisory Group] and CINCPAC. My own feeling is that the initial size should not exceed about 8000, of which a preponderant number would be in logistical-type units. After acquiring experience in operating in SVN, this initial force will require reorganization and adjustment to the local scene.

As CINCPAC will point out, any forces committed to SVN will need to be replaced by additional forces to his area from the stategic reserve in the U.S. Also, any troops to SVN are in addition to those which may be required to execute SEATO Plan 5 in Laos. Both facts should be taken into account in current considerations of the FY [fiscal year] 1963 budget which bear upon the permanent increase which should be made in the U.S. military establishment to maintain our strategic position for the long pull.

5 "The Situation Is Very Disturbing": The McNamara Report, 1963

Secretary of Defense Robert McNamara to President Johnson, 21 December 1963, reporting on problems identified during a two-day visit to South Vietnam.

In accordance with your request this morning, this is a summary of my conclusions after my visit to Vietnam on December 19–20.

1. *Summary* The situation is very disturbing. Current trends, unless reversed in the next 2–3 months, will lead to neutralization at best and more likely to a Communist-controlled state.

2. *The new government* is the greatest source of concern. It is indecisive and drifting. Although Minh states that he, rather than the Committee of Generals, is making decisions, it is not clear that this is actually so. In any event, neither he nor the Committee are experienced in political administration and so far they show little talent for it. There is no clear concept on how to re-shape or conduct the strategic hamlet program; the Province Chiefs, most of whom are new and inexperienced, are receiving little or no direction because the generals are so preoccupied with essentially political affairs. A specific example of the present situation is that General [name illegible] is spending little or no time commanding III Corps, which is in the vital zone around Saigon and needs full-time direction. I made these points as strongly as possible to Minh, Don, Kim, and Tho.

3. *The Country Team* is the second major weakness. It lacks leadership, has been poorly informed, and is not working to a common plan. A recent example of confusion had been conflicting USOM [United States Operations Mission] and military recommendations both to the Government of Vietnam and to Washington on the size of the military budget. Above all, Lodge has virtually no official contact with Harkins. Lodge sends in reports with major military implications without showing them to Harkins, and does not show Harkins important incoming traffic. My impression is that Lodge simply does not know how to conduct a coordinated administration. This has of course been stressed to him both by Dean Rusk and myself (and also by John McCone), and I do not think he is consciously rejecting our advice; he has just operated as a loner all his life and cannot readily change now. . . .

4. *Viet Cong progress* has been great during the period since the coup, with my best guess being that the situation has in fact been deteriorating in the countryside since July to a far greater extent than we realized because of our undue dependence on distorted Vietnamese reporting. The Viet Cong now control very high proportions of the people in certain key provinces, particularly those directly south and west of Saigon. The Strategic Hamlet Program was seriously over-extended in those provinces, and the Viet Cong has been able to destroy many hamlets, while others have been abandoned or in some cases betrayed or pillaged by the government's own Self-Defense Corps. In

these key provinces, the Viet Cong have destroyed almost all major roads, and are collecting taxes at will.

As remedial measures, we must get the government to reallocate its military forces so that its effective strength in these provinces is essentially doubled. We also need to have major increases in both military and USOM staffs, to sizes that will give us a reliable, independent U.S. appraisal of the status of operations. Thirdly, realistic pacification plans must be prepared, allocating adequate time to secure the remaining government-controlled areas and work out from there.

This gloomy picture prevails predominantly in the provinces around the capital and in the Delta action to accomplish each of these objectives was started while we were in Saigon. The situation in the northern and central areas is considerably better, and does not seem to have deteriorated substantially in recent months. General Harkins still hopes these areas may be made reasonably secure by the latter half of next year. . . .

5. *Infiltration* of men and equipment from North Vietnam continues using (a) land corridors through Laos and Cambodia; (b) the Mekong River waterways from Cambodia; (c) some possible entry from the sea and the tip of the Delta. The best guess is that 1000–1500 Viet Cong cadres entered South Vietnam from Laos in the first nine months of 1963. The Mekong route (and also the possible sea entry) is apparently used for heavier weapons and ammunition and raw materials which have been turning up in increasing numbers in the south and of which we have captured a few shipments. . . .

6. *Plans for Covert Action into North Vietnam* were prepared as we had requested and were an excellent job. They present a wide variety of sabotage and psychological operations against North Vietnam from which I believe we should aim to select those that provide maximum pressure with minimum risk. In accordance with your direction at the meeting, General Krulak of the JCS is chairing a group that will lay out a program in the next ten days for your consideration. . . .

6 The Tonkin Gulf Incident: President Lyndon Johnson Addresses Congress, 1964

The Tonkin Gulf Incident; 1964

President Johnson's Message to Congress

1. President Johnson's Message to Congress August 5, 1964

Last night I announced to the American people that the North Vietnamese regime had conducted further deliberate attacks against U.S. naval vessels operating in international waters, and I had therefore directed air action against gunboats and supporting facilities used in these hostile operations. This air action has now been carried out with substantial damage to the boats and facilities. Two U.S. aircraft were lost in the action.

After consultation with the leaders of both parties in the Congress, I further announced a decision to ask the Congress for a resolution expressing the unity and determination of the United States in supporting freedom and in protecting peace in southeast Asia.

These latest actions of the North Vietnamese regime has given a new and grave turn to the already serious situation in southeast Asia. Our commitments in that area are well known to the Congress. They were first made in 1954 by President Eisenhower. They were further defined in the Southeast Asia Collective Defense Treaty approved by the Senate in February 1955.

This treaty with its accompanying protocol obligates the United States and other members to act in accordance with their constitutional processes to meet Communist aggression against any of the parties or protocol states.

Our policy in southeast Asia has been consistent and unchanged since 1954. I summarized it on June 2 in four simple propositions:

America keeps her word. Here as elsewhere, we must and shall honor our commitments.

The issue is the future of southeast Asia as a whole. A threat to any nation in that region is a threat to all, and a threat to us.

Our purpose is peace. We have no military, political, or territorial ambitions in the area.

This is not just a jungle war, but a struggle for freedom on every front of human activity. Our military and economic assistance to South Vietnam and Laos in particular has the purpose of helping these countries to repel aggression and strengthen their independence.

The threat to the free nations of southeast Asia has long been clear. The North Vietnamese regime has constantly sought to take over South Vietnam and Laos. This Communist regime has violated the Geneva accords for Vietnam. It has systematically conducted a campaign of subversion, which includes the direction, training, and supply of personnel and arms for the conduct of guerrilla warfare in South Vietnamese territory. In Laos, the North Vietnamese regime has maintained military forces, used Laotian territory for infiltration into South Vietnam, and most recently carried out combat operations - all in direct violation of the Geneva Agreements of 1962.

In recent months, the actions of the North Vietnamese regime have become steadily more threatening . . .

As President of the United States I have concluded that I should now ask the Congress, on its part, to join in affirming the national determination that all such attacks will be met, and that the United States will continue in its basic policy of assisting the free nations of the area to defend their freedom.

As I have repeatedly made clear, the United States intends no rashness, and seeks no wider war. We must make it clear to all that the United States is united in its determination to bring about the end of Communist subversion and aggression in the area. We seek the full and effective restoration of the international agreements signed in Geneva in 1954, with respect to South Vietnam, and again in Geneva in 1962, with respect to Laos . . .

7 The Tonkin Gulf Resolution, 1964

Eighty-eighth Congress of the United States of America
AT THE SECOND SESSION

Begun and held at the City of Washington on Tuesday, the seventh day of January, one thousand nine hundred and sixty-four

Joint Resolution
To promote the maintenance of international peace and security in southeast Asia.

Whereas naval units of the Communist regime in Vietnam, in violation of the principles of the Charter of the United Nations and of international law, have deliberately and repeatedly attacked United Stated naval vessels lawfully present in international waters, and have thereby created a serious threat to international peace; and

Whereas these attackers are part of deliberate and systematic campaign of aggression that the Communist regime in North Vietnam has been waging against its neighbors and the nations joined with them in the collective defense of their freedom; and

Whereas the United States is assisting the peoples of southeast Asia to protest their freedom and has no territorial, military or political ambitions in that area, but desires only that these people should be left in peace to work out their destinies in their own way: Now, therefore be it

Resolved by the Senate and House of Representatives of the United States of America in Congress assembled, That the Congress approves and supports the determination of the President, as Commander in Chief, to take all necessary measures to repel any armed attack against the forces of the United States and to prevent further aggression.

Section 2. The United States regards as vital to its national interest and to world peace the maintenance of international peace and security in southeast Asia. Consonant with the Constitution of the United States and the Charter of the United Nations and in accordance with its obligations under the Southeast Asia Collective Defense Treaty, the United States is, therefore, prepared, as the President determines, to take all necessary steps, including the use of armed force, to assist any member or protocol state of the Southeast Asia Collective Defense Treaty requesting assistance in defense of its freedom.

Section 3. This resolution shall expire when the President shall determine that the peace and security of the area is reasonably assured by international conditions created by action of the United Nations or otherwise, except that it may be terminated earlier by concurrent resolution of the Congress.

8 "American Wars Have to Be Politically Understandable": Vice President Hubert Humphrey Opposes Expansion of the War, 1965

Memorandum from Vice President Hubert H. Humphrey to Johnson, 17 February 1965, in which Humphrey warns against Americanizing the war.

Washington, February 17, 1965.

SUBJECT Vietnam

I would like to share with you my views on the political consequences of certain courses of action that have been proposed in regard to U.S. policy in Southeast Asia. I refer both to the domestic political consequences here in the United States and to the international political consequences.

A. Domestic Political Consequences.

1. *1964 Campaign.*

Although the question of U.S. involvement in Vietnam is and should be a non-partisan question, there have always been significant differences in approach to the Asian question between the Republican Party and the Democratic Party. These came out in the 1964 campaign. The Republicans represented both by Goldwater, and the top Republican leaders in Congress, favored a quick, total military solution in Vietnam, to be achieved through military escalation of the war.

The Democratic position emphasized the complexity of a Vietnam situation involving both political, social and military factors; the necessity of staying in Vietnam as long as necessary; recognition that the war will be won or lost chiefly in South Vietnam.

In Vietnam, as in Korea, the Republicans have attacked the Democrats either for failure to use our military power to 'win' a total victory, or alternatively for losing the country to the Communists. The Democratic position has always been one of firmness in the face of Communist pressure but restraint in the use of military force; it has sought to obtain the best possible settlement without provoking a nuclear World War III; it has sought to leave open face-saving options to an opponent when necessary to avoid a nuclear show-down. When grave risks have been necessary, as in the case of Cuba, they have been taken. But here again a face-saving option was permitted the opponent. In all instances the Democratic position has included a balancing of both political and military factors.

Today the Administration is being charged by some of its critics with adopting the Goldwater position on Vietnam. While this is not true of the Administration's position as defined by the President, it is true that many key advisors in the Government are advocating a policy markedly similar to the Republican policy as defined by Goldwater.

2. *Consequences for other policies advocated by a Democratic Administration.*

The Johnson Administration is associated both at home and abroad with a policy of progress toward détente with the Soviet bloc, a policy of limited arms control, and a policy of new initiatives for peace. A full-scale military attack on North Vietnam—with the attendant risk of an open military clash with Communist China—would risk gravely undermining other U.S. policies. It would eliminate for the time being any possible exchange between the President and Soviet leaders; it would postpone any progress on arms control; it would encourage the Soviet Union and China to end their rift; it would seriously hamper our efforts to strengthen relations with our European allies; it would weaken our position in the United Nations; it might require a call-up of reservists if we were to get involved in a large-scale land war—and a consequent increase in defense expenditures; it would tend to shift the Administration's emphasis from its Great Society oriented programs to further military outlays; finally and most important it would damage the image of the President of the United States—and that of the United States itself.

3. *Involvement in a full scale war with North Vietnam would not make sense to the majority of the American people.*

American wars have to be politically understandable by the American public. There has to be a cogent, convincing case if we are to have sustained public support. In World Wars I and II we had this. In Korea we were moving under UN auspices to defend South Korea against dramatic, across-the-border conventional aggression. Yet even with those advantages, we could not sustain American political support for fighting the Chinese in Korea in 1952.

Today in Vietnam we lack the very advantages we had in Korea. The public is worried and confused. Our rationale for action has shifted away now even from the notion that we are there as advisors on request of a free government—to the simple argument of our 'national interest.' We have not succeeded in making this 'national interest' interesting enough at home or abroad to generate support.

4. From a political viewpoint, the American people find it hard to understand why we risk World War III by enlarging a war under terms we found unacceptable 12 years ago in Korea, particularly since the chances of success are slimmer.

Politically, people think of North Vietnam and North Korea. They recall all the 'lessons' of 1950–53:

a. The limitations of air power.

b. The Chinese intervention.

c. The 'never again club'—never again GI's fighting a land war against Asians in Asia.

d. The Eisenhower Administration's compromise which represented a frank recognition of all these factors.

If a war with China was ruled out by the Truman and Eisenhower Administrations alike in 1952–3, at a time when we alone had nuclear weapons, people find it hard to contemplate such a war with China now. No one really believes the Soviet Union would allow us to destroy Communist China with nuclear weapons, as Russia's status as a world power would be undermined if she did.

5. *Absence of confidence in the Government of South Vietnam.*

Politically, people can't understand why we would run grave risks to support a country which is totally unable to put its own house in order. The chronic instability in Saigon directly undermines American political support for our policy.

6. Politically, it is hard to justify over a long period of time sustained, large-scale U.S. air bombardments across a border as a response to camouflaged, often non-sensational, elusive, small-scale terror which has been going on for 10 years in what looks like a civil war in the South.

7. Politically, in Washington and across the country, the opposition is more Democratic than Republican.

8. Politically, it is always hard to cut losses. But the Johnson Administration is in a stronger position to do so than any Administration in this century. 1965 is the year of minimum political risk for the Johnson Administration. Indeed it is the first year when we can face the Vietnam problem without being preoccupied with the political repercussions from the Republican right. As indicated earlier, the political problems are likely to come from new and different sources if we pursue an enlarged military policy very long (Democratic liberals, Independents, Labor, Church groups).

9. Politically, we now risk creating the impression that we are the prisoner of events in Vietnam. This blurs the Administration's leadership role and has spill-over effects across the board. It also helps erode confidence and credibility in our policies.

10. The President is personally identified with, and admired for, political ingenuity. He will be expected to put all his great political sense to work now for international political solutions. People will be counting upon him to use on the world scene his unrivalled talents as a political leader.

They will be watching to see how he makes this transition. The best possible outcome a year from now would be a Vietnam settlement which turns out to be better than was in the cards because the President's political talents for the first time came to grips with a fateful world crisis and so successfully. It goes without saying that the subsequent domestic political benefits of such an outcome, and such a new dimension for the President, would be enormous.

11. If on the other hand, we find ourselves leading from frustration to escalation, and end up short of a war with China but embroiled deeper in fighting with Vietnam over the next few months, political opposition will steadily mount. It will underwrite all the negativism and disillusionment which we already have about foreign involvement generally—with direct spill-over effects politically for all the Democratic internationalist programs

to which we are committed—AID, UN, disarmament, and activist world policies generally.

B. International Political Implications of Vietnam

1. What is our goal, our ultimate objective in Vietnam? Is our goal to restore a military balance between North and South Vietnam so as to go to the conference table later to negotiate a settlement? I believe it is the latter. If so, what is the optimum time for achieving the most favorable combination of factors to achieve this goal?

If ultimately a negotiated settlement is our aim, when do we start developing a *political track, in addition to the military one*, that might lead us to the conference table? I believe we should develop the political track earlier rather than later. We should take the initiative on the political side and not end up being dragged to a conference as an unwilling participant. This does not mean we should cease all programs of military pressure. But we should distinguish carefully between those military actions necessary to reach our political goal of a negotiated settlement, and those likely to provoke open Chinese military intervention.

We should not underestimate the likelihood of Chinese intervention and repeat the mistake of the Korean War. If we begin to bomb further north in Vietnam, the likelihood is great of an encounter with the Chinese Air Force operating from sanctuary bases across the border. Once the Chinese Air Force is involved, Peking's full prestige will be involved as she cannot afford to permit her Air Force to be destroyed. To do so would undermine, if not end, her role as a great power in Asia.

Confrontation with the Chinese Air Force can easily lead to massive retaliation by the Chinese in South Vietnam. What is our response to this? Do we bomb Chinese air bases and nuclear installations? If so, will not the Soviet Union honor its treaty of friendship and come to China's assistance? I believe there is a good chance that it would—thereby involving us in a war with both China and the Soviet Union. Here again, we must remember the consequences for the Soviet Union of *not* intervening if China's military power is destroyed by the U.S.

9 President Richard Nixon's "Silent Majority Speech," 1969

This speech, delivered by President Richard Nixon on 3 November 1969, appealed to the American public at a time of considerable antiwar activity.

In January I could only conclude that the precipitate withdrawal of American forces from Vietnam would be a disaster not only for South Vietnam but for the United States and for the cause of peace.

For the South Vietnamese, our precipitate withdrawal would inevitably allow the Communists to repeat the massacres which followed their takeover in the North 15 years before. . . .

For the United States, this first defeat in our Nation's history would result in a collapse of confidence in American leadership, not only in Asia but throughout the world. . . .

For these reasons, I rejected the recommendation that I should end the war by immediately withdrawing all of our forces. I chose instead to change American policy on both the negotiating front and battlefront. . . .

It has become clear that the obstacle in negotiating an end to the war is not the President of the United States. It is not the South Vietnamese Government.

The obstacle is the other side's absolute refusal to show the least willingness to join us in seeking a just peace. And it will not do so while it is convinced that all it has to do is to wait for our next concession, and our next concession after that one, until it gets everything it wants.

There can now be no longer any question that progress in negotiation depends only on Hanoi's deciding to negotiate, to negotiate seriously. . . .

At the time we launched our search for peace I recognized we might not succeed in bringing an end to the war through negotiation. I, therefore, put into effect another plan to bring peace—a plan which will bring the war to an end regardless of what happens on the negotiating front. . . .

In the previous administration, we Americanized the war in Vietnam. In this administration, we are Vietnamizing the search for peace. . . .

The Vietnamization plan was launched following Secretary Laird's visit to Vietnam in March. Under the plan, I ordered first a substantial increase in the training and equipment of South Vietnamese forces.

In July, on my visit to Vietnam, I changed General Abrams' orders so that they were consistent with the objectives of our new policies. Under the new orders, the primary mission of our troops is to enable the South Vietnamese forces to assume the full responsibility for the security of South Vietnam. . . .

We have adopted a plan which we have worked out in cooperation with the South Vietnamese for the complete withdrawal of all US combat ground forces, and their replacement by South Vietnamese forces on an orderly scheduled timetable. This withdrawal will be made from strength and not from weakness. As South Vietnamese forces become stronger, the rate of American withdrawal can become greater. . . .

For almost 200 years, the policy of this Nation has been made under our Constitution by those leaders in the Congress and the White House elected by all of the people. If a vocal minority, however fervent its cause, prevails over reason and the will of the majority, this Nation has no future as a free society. . . .

Two hundred years ago this Nation was weak and poor. But even then, America was the hope of millions in the world. Today we have become the strongest and richest nation in the world. And the wheel of destiny has turned so that any hope the world has for the survival of peace and freedom will be determined by whether the American people have the moral stamina and the courage to meet the challenge of free world leadership.

Let historians not record that when America was the most powerful nation in the world we passed on the other side of the road and allowed the last hopes for peace and freedom of millions of people to be suffocated by the forces of totalitarianism.

And so tonight—to you, the great silent majority of my fellow Americans—I ask for your support.

I pledged in my campaign for the Presidency to end the war in a way that we could win the peace. I have initiated a plan of action which will enable me to keep that pledge.

The more support I can have from the American people, the sooner that pledge can be redeemed; for the more divided we are at home, the less likely the enemy is to negotiate at Paris.

Let us be united for peace. Let us also be united against defeat. Because let us understand: North Vietnam cannot defeat or humiliate the United States. Only Americans can do that. . . .

10 President Richard Nixon Explains the American Invasion of Cambodia, 1970

THE INVASION OF CAMBODIA

Televised speech delivered by President Richard Nixon on 30 April 1970 to explain the US and South Vietnamese offensive into Cambodia.

I have concluded that the actions of the enemy in the last 10 days clearly endanger the lives of Americans who are in Vietnam now and would constitute an unacceptable risk to those who will be there after withdrawal of another 150,000. . . .

For 5 years, neither the United States nor South Vietnam has moved against these enemy sanctuaries because we did not wish to violate the territory of a neutral nation. Even after the Vietnamese Communists began to expand these sanctuaries 4 weeks ago, we counseled patience to our South Vietnamese allies and imposed restraints on our own commanders. . . .

In cooperation with the armed forces of South Vietnam, attacks are being launched this week to clean out major enemy sanctuaries on the Cambodian–Vietnam border. . . .

Tonight, American and South Vietnamese units will attack the headquarters for the entire Communist military operation in South Vietnam. This key control center has been occupied by the North Vietnamese and Vietcong for 5 years in blatant violation of Cambodian neutrality.

This is not an invasion of Cambodia. The areas in which these attacks will be launched are completely occupied and controlled by North Vietnamese forces. Our purpose is not to occupy the areas. Once enemy forces are driven out of these sanctuaries and once their military supplies are destroyed, we will withdraw. . . .

My fellow Americans, we live in an age of anarchy, both abroad and at home. We see mindless attacks on all the great institutions which have been created by free civilizations in the last 500 years. Even here in the United States, great universities are being systematically destroyed. . . .

If, when the chips are down, the world's most powerful nation, the United States of America, acts like a pitiful, helpless giant, the forces of totalitarianism and anarchy will threaten free nations and free institutions throughout the world.

It is not our power but our will and character that is being tested tonight. . . .

11 "We Feel We Have Been Used in the Worst Fashion": John Kerry Testifies on the Vietnam War, 1971

Mr. Kerry. Thank you very much, Senator Fulbright, Senator Javits, Senator Symington, Senator Pell. I would like to say for the record, and also for the men behind me who are also wearing the uniform and their medals, that my sitting here is really symbolic. I am not here as John Kerry. I am here as one member of the group of 1,000, which is a small representation of a very much larger group of veterans in this country, and were it possible for all of them to sit at this table they would be here and have the same kind of testimony. . . .

I would like to talk to you a little bit about what the result is of the feelings these men carry with them after coming back from Vietnam. The country doesn't know it yet but it has created a monster, a monster in the form of millions of men who have been taught to deal and to trade in violence and who are given the chance to die for the biggest nothing in history; men who have returned with a sense of anger and a sense of betrayal which no one has yet grasped.

As a veteran and one who feels this anger I would like to talk about it. We are angry because we feel we have been used in the worst fashion by the administration of this country.

In 1970 at West Point Vice President Agnew said "some glamorize the criminal misfits of society while our best men die in Asian rice paddies to preserve the freedom which most of those misfits abuse," and this was used as a rallying point for our effort in Vietnam.

But for us, as boys in Asia whom the country was supposed to support, his statement is a terrible distortion from which we can only draw a very deep sense of revulsion, and hence the anger of some of the men who are here in Washington today. It is a distortion because we in no way consider ourselves the best men of this country; because those he calls misfits were standing up for us in a way that nobody else in this country dared to; because so many who have died would have returned to this country to join the misfits in their efforts to ask for an immediate withdrawal from South Vietnam; because so many of those best men have returned as quadruplegics and amputees—and they lie forgotten in Veterans Administration Hospitals in this country which fly the flag which so many have chosen as their own personal symbol—and we cannot consider ourselves America's best men when we are ashamed of and hated for what we were called on to do in Southeast Asia.

In our opinion, and from our experience, there is nothing in South Vietnam which could happen that realistically threatens the United States of America. And to attempt to justify the loss of one American life in Vietnam, Cambodia or Laos by linking such loss to the preservation of freedom, which those misfits supposedly abuse, is to us the height of criminal hypocrisy, and it is that kind of hypocrisy which we feel has torn this country apart. . . .

We are probably angriest about all that we were told about Vietnam and about the mystical war against communism. We found that not only was it a civil war, an effort by a people who had for years been seeking their liberation from any colonial influence whatsoever, but also we found that the Vietnamese whom we had enthusiastically molded after our own image were hard put to take up the fight against the threat we were supposedly saving them from.

We found most people didn't even know the difference between communism and democracy. They only wanted to work in rice paddies without helicopters strafing them and bombs with napalm burning their villages and tearing their country apart. They wanted everything to do with the war, particularly with this foreign presence of the United States of America, to leave them alone in peace, and they practiced the art of survival by siding with whichever military force was present at a particular time, be it Viet Cong, North Vietnamese or American.

We found also that all too often American men were dying in those rice paddies for want of support from their allies. We saw first hand how monies from American taxes were used for a corrupt dictatorial regime. We saw that many people in this country had a one-sided idea of who was kept free by our flag, and blacks provided the highest percentage of casualties. We saw Vietnam ravaged equally by American bombs and search and destroy missions, as well as by Viet Cong terrorism, and yet we listened while this country tried to blame all of the havoc on the Viet Cong.

We rationalized destroying villages in order to save them. We saw America lose her sense of morality as she accepted very coolly a My Lai and refused to give up the image of American soldiers who hand out chocolate bars and chewing gum.

We learned the meaning of free fire zones, shooting anything that moves, and we watched while America placed a cheapness on the lives of orientals.

We watched the United States falsification of body counts. We listened while month after month we were told the back of the enemy was about to break. We fought using weapons against "oriental human beings." We fought using weapons against those people which I do not believe this country would dream of using were we fighting in the European theater. We watched while men charged up hills because a general said that hill has to be taken, and after losing one platoon or two platoons they marched away to leave the hill for reoccupation by the North Vietnamese. We watched pride allow the most unimportant battles to be blown into extravaganzas, because we couldn't lose, and we couldn't retreat, and because it didn't matter how many American bodies were lost to prove that point, and so there were Hamburger Hills and Khe Sahns and Hill 81s and Fire Base 6s, and so many others.

Now we are told that the men who fought there must watch quietly while American lives are lost so that we can exercise the incredible arrogance of Vietnamizing the Vietnamese. Each day to facilitate the process by which the United States washes her hands of Vietnam someone has to give up his life so that the United States doesn't have to admit something that the entire world already knows, so that we can't say that we have made a mistake. Someone has to die so that President Nixon won't be, and these are his words, "the first President to lose a war."

We are asking Americans to think about that because how do you ask a man to be the last man to die in Vietnam? How do you ask a man to be the last man to die for a mistake? But we are trying to do that, and we are doing it with thousands of rationalizations, and if you read carefully the President's last speech to the people of this country, you can see that he says, and says clearly, "but the issue, gentlemen, the issue, is communism, and the question is whether or not we will leave that country to the communists or whether or not we will try to give it hope to be a free people." But the point is they are not a free people now under us. They are not a free people, and we cannot fight communism all over the world. I think we should have learned that lesson by now. . . .

Suddenly we are faced with a very sickening situation in this country, because there is no moral indignation and, if there is, it comes from people who are almost exhausted by their past indignations. . . . The country seems to have lain down and shrugged off something as serious as Laos, just as we calmly shrugged off the loss of 700,000 lives in Pakistan, the so-called greatest disaster of all times.

But we are here as veterans to say we think we are in the midst of the greatest disaster of all times now, because they are still dying over there—not just Americans, but Vietnamese—and we are rationalizing leaving that country so that those people can go on killing each other for years to come.

Americans seem to have accepted the idea that the war is winding down, at least for Americans, and they have also allowed the bodies which were once used by a President for statistics to prove that we were winning that war, to be used as evidence against a man who followed orders and who interpreted those orders no differently than hundreds of other men in Vietnam.

We veterans can only look with amazement on the fact that this country has been unable to see there is absolutely no difference between ground troops and a helicopter crew, and yet people have accepted a differentiation fed them by the administration.

No ground troops are in Laos so it is all right to kill Laotians by remote control. But believe me the helicopter crews fill the same body bags and they wreak the same kind of damage on the Vietnamese and Laotian countryside as anybody else, and the President is talking about allowing that to go on for many years to come. One can only ask if we will really be satisfied only when the troops march into Hanoi.

We are asking here in Washington for some action; action from the Congress of the United States of America which has the power to raise and maintain armies, and which by the Constitution also has the power to declare war. We have come here, not to the President, because we believe that this body can be responsive to the will of the people, and we believe that the will of the people says that we should be out of Vietnam now.

We are here in Washington also to say that the problem of this war is not just a question of war and diplomacy. It is part and parcel of everything that we are trying as human beings to communicate to people in this country—the question of racism, which is rampant in the military, and so many other questions such as the use of weapons; the hypocrisy in our taking umbrage in the Geneva Conventions and using that as justification for a continuation of this war when we are more guilty than any other body of violations of those Geneva Conventions; in the use of free fire zones, harassment interdiction fire, search and destroy missions, the bombings, the torture of prisoners, the killing of prisoners, all accepted policy by many units in South Vietnam. That is what we are trying to say. . . .

We are also here to ask, and we are here to ask vehemently, where are the leaders of our country? Where is the leadership? We are here to ask where are McNamara, Rostow, Bundy, Gilpatric and so many others? Where are they now that we, the men whom they sent off to war, have returned? These are commanders who have deserted their troops, and there is no more serious crime in the law of war. The Army says they never leave their wounded. The Marines say they never leave even their dead. These men have left all the casualties and retreated behind a pious shield of public rectitude. They have left the real stuff of their reputations bleaching behind them in the sun in this country.

Finally, this administration has done us the ultimate dishonor. They have attempted to disown us and the sacrifices we made for this country. In their blindness and fear they have tried to deny that we are veterans or that we served in Nam. We do not need their testimony. Our own scars and stumps of limbs are witness enough for others and for ourselves.

We wish that a merciful God could wipe away our own memories of that service as easily as this administration has wiped away their memories of us. But all that they have done all that they can do by this denial is to make more clear than ever our own determination to undertake one last mission—to search out and destroy the last vestige of this barbaric war, to pacify our own hearts, to conquer the hate and the fear that have driven this country these last ten years and more. So when 30 years from now our brothers go down the street without a leg, without an arm, or a face, and small boys ask why, we will be able to say "Vietnam" and not mean a desert, nor a filthy obscene memory, but mean instead the place where America finally turned and where soldiers like us helped it in the turning.

Thank you.

12 The War Powers Act, 1973

In the absence of a declaration of war, in any case in which United States Armed Forces are introduced—

(1) into hostilities or into situations where imminent involvement in hostilities is clearly indicated by the circumstances;
(2) into the territory, airspace or waters of a foreign nation, while equipped for combat, except for deployments which relate solely to supply, replacement, repair or training of such forces; or
(3) in numbers which substantially enlarge United States Armed Forces equipped for combat already located in a foreign nation;

the President shall submit within 48 hours to the Speaker of the House of Representatives and to the President, pro tempore of the Senate a report, in writing, setting forth—

(A) the circumstances necessitating the introduction of United States Armed Forces;
(B) the constitutional and legislative authority under which such introduction took place; and
(C) the estimated scope and duration of the hostilities or involvement. . . . The President shall provide such other information as the Congress may request in the fulfillment of its constitutional responsibilities with respect to committing the Nation to war and to the use of United States Armed Forces abroad.

Whenever United States Armed Forces are introduced into hostilities . . . the President shall, so long as such armed forces continue to be engaged in such hostilities or situation, report to the Congress periodically on the status of such hostilities or situation as well as on the scope and duration of such hostilities or situation, but in no event shall he report to the Congress less often than once every six months.

1544. Congressional action. . . .

(*b*) *Termination of use of United States Armed Forces; exceptions; extension period.* Within sixty calendar days after a report is submitted or is required to be submitted pursuant to section 1543(a)(1) of this title, whichever is earlier, the President shall terminate any use of United States Armed Forces with respect to which such report was submitted (or required to be submitted), unless the Congress (1) has declared war or has enacted a specific authorization for such use of United States Armed Forces, (2) has extended by law such sixty-day period, or (3) is physically unable to meet as a result of an armed attack upon the

United States. Such sixty-day period shall be extended for not more than an additional thirty days if the President determines and certifies to the Congress in writing that unavoidable military necessity respecting the safety of United States Armed Forces requires the continued use of such armed forces in the course of bringing about a prompt removal of such forces.

(c) *Concurrent resolution for removal by President of United States Armed Forces.* Not-withstanding subsection (b) of this section, at any time that United States Armed Forces are engaged in hostilities outside the territory of the United States, its possessions and territories without a declaration of war or specific statutory authorization, such forces shall be removed by the President if the Congress so directs by concurrent resolution.

Section 5

Many Voices, Many Directions
1970s–Present

1 "But We Won't Be Silent Anymore": Gloria Steinem Testifies on the Equal Rights Amendment, 1970

During 12 years of working for a living, I have experienced much of the legal and social discrimination reserved for women in this country. I have been refused service in public restaurants, ordered out of public gathering places, and turned away from apartment rentals; all for the clearly-stated, sole reason that I am a woman. And all without the legal remedies available to blacks and other minorities. I have been excluded from professional groups, writing assignments on so-called "unfeminine" subjects such as politics, full participation in the Democratic Party, jury duty, and even from such small male privileges as discounts on airline fares. Most important to me, I have been denied a society in which women are encouraged, or even allowed to think of themselves as first-class citizens and responsible human beings.

However, after 2 years of researching the status of American women, I have discovered that in reality, I am very, very lucky. Most women, both wage-earners and housewives, routinely suffer more humiliation and injustice than I do.

As a freelance writer, I don't work in the male-dominated hierarchy of an office. (Women, like blacks and other visibly different minorities, do better in individual professions such as the arts, sports, or domestic work; anything in which they don't have authority over white males.) I am not one of the millions of women who must support a family. Therefore, I haven't had to go on welfare because there are no day-care centers for my children while I work, and I haven't had to submit to the humiliating welfare inquiries about my private and sexual life, inquiries from which men are exempt. I haven't had to brave the sex bias of labor unions and employers, only to see my family subsist on a median salary 40 percent less than the male median salary.

I hope this committee will hear the personal, daily injustices suffered by many women-professionals and day laborers, women house-bound by welfare as well as by suburbia. We have all been silent for too long. But we won't be silent anymore.

The truth is that all our problems stem from the same sex based myths. We may appear before you as white radicals or the middle-aged middle-class or black soul sisters, but we are all sisters in fighting against these outdated myths. Like racial myths, they have been reflected in our laws. Let me list a few.

That woman are biologically inferior to men. In fact, an equally good case can be made for the reverse. Women live longer than men, even when the men are not subject to business pressures. Women survived Nazi concentration camps better, keep cooler heads in emergencies currently studied by disaster-researchers, are protected against heart attacks by their female sex hormones, and are so much more durable at every stage of life that nature must conceive 20 to 50 percent more males in order to keep the balance going.

Man's hunting activities are forever being pointed to as tribal proof of superiority. But while he was hunting, women built houses, tilled the fields, developed animal husbandry, and perfected language. Men, being all alone in the bush, often developed into a creature as strong as women, fleeter of foot, but not very bright.

However, I don't want to prove the superiority of one sex to another. That would only be repeating a male mistake. English scientists once definitively proved, after all, that the English were descended from the angels, while the Irish were descended from the apes; it was the rationale for England's domination of Ireland for more than a century. The point is that science is used to support current myth and economics almost as much as the church was.

What we do know is that the difference between two races or two sexes is much smaller than the differences to be found within each group. Therefore, in spite of the slide show on female inferiorities that I understand was shown to you yesterday, the law makes much more sense when it treats individuals, not groups bundled together by some condition of birth.

•••

Another myth, that women are already treated equally in this society. I am sure there has been ample testimony to prove that equal pay for equal work, equal chance for advancement, and equal training or encouragement is obscenely scarce in every field, even those—like food and fashion industries—that are supposedly "feminine."

A deeper result of social and legal injustice, however, is what sociologists refer to as "Internalized Aggression." Victims of aggression absorb the myth of their own inferiority, and come to believe that their group is in fact second class. Even when they themselves realize they are not second class, they may still think their group is, thus the tendency to be the only Jew in the club, the only black woman on the block, the only woman in the office.

Women suffer this second class treatment from the moment they are born. They are expected to be, rather than achieve, to function biologically rather than learn. A brother, whatever his intellect, is more likely to get the family's encouragement and education money, while girls are often pressured to conceal ambition and intelligence. . . .

Teachers, parents, and the Supreme Court may exude a protective, well-meaning rationale, but limiting the individual's ambition is doing no one a favor. Certainly not this country; it needs all the talent it can get.

Another myth, that American women hold great economic power. Fifty-one percent of all shareholders in this country are women. That is a favorite male-chauvinist statistic. However, the number of shares they hold is so small that the total is only 18 percent of all the shares. Even those holdings are often controlled by men.

Similarly, only 5 percent of all the people in the country who receive $10,000 a year or more, earned or otherwise, are women. And that includes the famous rich widows.

The constantly repeated myth of our economic power seems less testimony to our real power than to the resentment of what little power we do have.

Another myth, that children must have full-time mothers. American mothers spend more time with their homes and children than those of any other society we know about. In the past, joint families, servants, a prevalent system in which grandparents raised the children, or family field work in the agrarian systems—all these factors contributed more to child care than the labor-saving devices of which we are so proud.

The truth is that most American children seem to be suffering from too much mother, and too little father. Part of the program of Women's Liberation is a return of fathers to their children. If laws permit women equal work and pay opportunities, men will then be relieved of their role as sole breadwinner. Fewer ulcers, fewer hours of meaningless work, equal responsibility for his own children: these are a few of the reasons that Women's Liberation is Men's Liberation too.

As for psychic health of the children, studies show that the quality of time spent by parents is more important than the quantity. The most damaged children were not those whose mothers worked, but those whose mothers preferred to work but stayed home out of the role-playing desire to be a "good mother."

Another myth, that the women's movement is not political, won't last, or is somehow not "serious." When black people leave their 19th century roles, they are feared. When women dare to leave theirs, they are ridiculed. We understand this; we accept the burden of ridicule. It won't keep us quiet anymore.

Similarly, it shouldn't deceive male observers into thinking that this is somehow a joke. We are 51 percent of the population; we are essentially united on these issues across boundaries of class or race or age; and we may well end by changing this society more than the civil rights movement. That is an apt parallel. We, too, have our right wing and left wing, our separatists, gradualists, and Uncle Toms. But we are changing our own consciousness, and that of the country. . . . Women's bodies will no longer be owned by the state for the production of workers and soldiers; birth control and abortion are facts of everyday life. The new family is an egalitarian family.

Gunnar Myrdal noted 30 years ago the parallel between women and Negroes in this country. Both suffered from such restricting social myths as: smaller brains, passive natures, inability to govern themselves (and certainly not white men), sex objects only, childlike natures, special skills, and the like. When evaluating a general statement about women, it might be valuable to substitute "black people" for "women"— just to test the prejudice at work.

And it might be valuable to do this constitutionally as well. Neither group is going to be content as a cheap labor pool anymore. And neither is going to be content without full constitutional rights.

Finally, I would like to say one thing about this time in which I am testifying. I had deep misgivings about discussing this topic when National Guardsmen are occupying our campuses, the country is being turned against itself in a terrible polarization, and America is enlarging an already inhuman and unjustifiable war. But it seems to me that much of the trouble in this country has to do with the "masculine mystique;" with the myth that masculinity somehow depends on the subjugation of other people. It is a bipartisan problem; both our past and current Presidents seem to be victims of this myth, and to behave accordingly.

Women are not more moral than men. We are only uncorrupted by power. But we do not want to imitate men, to join this country as it is, and I think our very participation will change it. Perhaps women elected leaders—and there will be many of them—will not be so likely to dominate black people or yellow people or men; anybody who looks different from us.

After all, we won't have our masculinity to prove.

2 "We Have a Cancer Within": President Richard Nixon and His Advisors Discuss the Watergate Scandal, 1973

D[ean]: The reason that I thought we ought to talk this morning is because in our conversations, I have the impression that you don't know everything I know and it makes it very difficult for you to make judgments that only you can make on some of these things and I thought that—

P[resident]: In other words, I have to know why you feel that we shouldn't unravel something?

D: Let me give you my overall first.

P: In other words, your judgment as to where it stands, and where we will go.

D: I think that there is no doubt about the seriousness of the problem we've got. We have a cancer within, close to the Presidency, that is growing. It is growing daily. It's compounded, growing geometrically now, because it compounds itself. That will be clear if I, you know, explain some of the details of why it is. Basically, it is because (1) we are being blackmailed; (2) people are going to start perjuring themselves very quickly that have not had to perjure themselves to protect other people in the line. And there is no assurance—

P: That that won't bust?

D: That that won't bust. So let me give you the sort of basic facts, talking first about the Watergate; and then about Segretti; and then about some of the peripheral items that have come up. First of all on the Watergate: how did it all start, where did it start? OK! It started with an instruction to me from Bob Haldeman to see if we couldn't set up a perfectly legitimate campaign intelligence operation over at the Re-Election Committee. . . . That is when I came up with Gordon Liddy. They needed a lawyer. Gordon had an intelligence background from his FBI service. I was aware of the fact that he had done some extremely sensitive things for the White House while he had been at the White House and he had apparently done them well. Going out into Ellsberg's doctor's office—

P: Oh, yeah.

D: And things like this. He worked with leaks. He tracked these things down. So the report that I got . . . was that he was a hell of a good man and not only that a good lawyer and could set up a proper operation. . . . Magruder called me in January and said I would like to have you come over and see Liddy's plan.

P: January of '72?

D: January of '72.

D: . . . So I came over and Liddy laid out a million dollar plan that was the most incredible thing I have ever laid my eyes on: all in codes, and involved black bag operations, kidnapping, providing prostitutes to weaken the opposition, bugging, mugging teams. It was just an incredible thing. . . .

So there was a second meeting. . . . I came into the tail end of the meeting. . . . [T]hey were discussing again bugging, kidnapping and the like. At this point I said right in front of everybody, very clearly, I said, "These are not the sort of things (1) that are ever to be discussed in the office of the Attorney General of the United States—that was where he still was—and I am personally incensed." And I am trying to get Mitchell off the hook. . . . So I let it be known. I said, "You all pack that stuff up and get it the hell out of here. You just can't talk this way in this office and you should re-examine your whole thinking."

P: Who all was present?

D: It was Magruder, Mitchell, Liddy and myself. I came back right after the meeting and told Bob, "Bob, we have a growing disaster on our hands if they are thinking this way," and I said, "The White House has got to stay out of this and I, frankly, am not going to be involved in it." He said, "I agree, John." I thought at that point that the thing was turned off. That is the last I heard of it and I thought it was turned off because it was an absurd proposal. . . . I think Bob was assuming that they had something that was proper over there, some intelligence gathering operation that Liddy was operating. . . . They were going to infiltrate, and bug, and do this sort of thing to a lot of these targets. This is knowledge I have after the fact. Apparently after they had initially broken in and bugged the DNC they were getting information. . . .

P: They had never bugged Muskie, though, did they?

D: No, they hadn't, but they had infiltrated it by a secretary.

P: By a secretary?

D: By a secretary and a chauffeur. There is nothing illegal about that. So the information was coming over here. . . . The next point in time that I became aware of anything was on June 17th when I got the word that there had been this break in at the DNC and somebody from our Committee had been caught in the DNC. And I said, "Oh, (expletive deleted)." You know, eventually putting the pieces together—

P: You knew what it was.

D: I knew who it was. . . .

P: Why at that point in time I wonder? I am just trying to think. We had just finished the Moscow trip.

The Democrats had just nominated [George] McGovern—I mean, (expletive deleted), what in the hell were these people doing? I can see their doing it earlier. I can see the pressures, but I don't see why all the pressure was on then.

D: I don't know, other than the fact that they might have been looking for information about the conventions.

P: That's right. . . .

P: What did they say in the Grand Jury?

D: They said, as they said before the trial in the Grand Jury, that . . . we knew [Liddy] had these capacities to do legitimate intelligence. We had no idea what he was doing. . . . We had no knowledge that he was going to bug the DNC.

P: The point is, that is not true?

D: That's right.

P: Magruder did know it was going to take place?

D: Magruder gave the instructions to be back in the DNC.

P: He did?

D: Yes.

P: You know that?

D: Yes.

P: I see. OK.

D: I honestly believe that no one over here knew that. I know that as God is my maker, I had no knowledge that they were going to do this.

P: Bob didn't either, or wouldn't have known that either. You are not the issue involved. Had Bob known, he would be.

D: Bob—I don't believe specifically knew that they were going in there.

P: I don't think so.

D: I don't think he did. I think he knew that there was a capacity to do this but he was not given the specific direction. . . .

D: So, those people are in trouble as a result of the Grand Jury and the trial. . . . Now what has happened post June 17? I was under pretty clear instructions not to investigate this, but this could have been disastrous on the electorate if all hell had broken loose. I worked on a theory of containment—

P: Sure.

D: To try to hold it right where it was.

P: Right.

D: There is no doubt that I was totally aware of what the Bureau was doing at all times. I was totally aware of what the Grand Jury was doing. I knew what witnesses were going to be called. I knew what they were asked, and I had to. . . . Now post June 17th: These guys . . . started making demands. "We have to have attorneys fees. We don't have any money ourselves, and you are asking us to take this through the election." Alright, so arrangements were made through Mitchell, initiating it. And I was present in discussions where these guys had to be taken care of. Their attorneys fees had to be done. Kalmbach was brought in. Kalmbach raised some cash.

P: They put that under the cover of a Cuban Committee, I suppose?

D: Well, they had a Cuban Committee and . . . some of it was given to Hunt's lawyer, who in turn passed it out. . . .

P: (unintelligible)— but I would certainly keep that cover for whatever it is worth. . . .

D: . . . Here is what is happening right now. . . . One, this is going to be a continual blackmail operation by Hunt and Liddy and the Cubans. No doubt about it. And McCord, . . . Hunt has now made a direct threat against Ehrlichman, . . . He says, "I will bring John Ehrlichman down to his knees and put him in jail. I have done enough seamy things for he and [Egil] Krogh, they'll never survive it."

P: Was he talking about Ellsberg?

D: Ellsberg, and apparently some other things. I don't know the full extent of it.

P: I don't know about anything else.

D: I don't know either, and I hate to learn some of these things. So that is that situation. Now, where are we at the soft points? How many people know about this? Well, let me go one step further in this whole thing. The Cubans that were used in the Watergate were also the same Cubans that Hunt and Liddy used for this California Ellsberg thing, for the break in out there. So they are aware of that. How high their knowledge is, is something else. Hunt and Liddy, of course, are totally aware of it, of the fact that it is right out of the White House.

P: I don't know what the hell we did that for!

D: I don't know either. . . . So that is it. That is the extent of the knowledge. So where are the soft spots on this? Well, first of all, there is the problem of the continued blackmail which will not only go on now, but it will go on while these people are in prison, and it will compound the obstruction of justice situation. It will cost money. It is dangerous. People around here are not pros at this sort of thing. This is the sort of thing Mafia people can do: washing money, getting clean money, and things like that. We just don't know about those things, because we are not criminals and not used to dealing in that business.

P: That's right.

D: It is a tough thing to know how to do.

P: Maybe it takes a gang to do that.

D: That's right. There is a real problem as to whether we could even do it. Plus there is a real problem in raising money. Mitchell has been working on raising some money. He is one of the ones with the most to lose. But there is no denying the fact that the White House, in Ehrlichman, Haldeman and Dean are involved in some of the early money decisions.

P: How much money do you need?

D: I would say these people are going to cost a million dollars over the next two years.

P: We could get that. On the money, if you need the money you could get that. You could get a million dollars. You could get it in cash. I know where it could be gotten. It is not easy, but it could be done. But the question is who the hell would handle it? Any ideas on that?. . .

D: Now we've got [Herbert] Kalmbach. Kalmbach received, at the close of the '68 campaign in January of 1969, he got a million $700,000 to be custodian for. That came, down from New York, and was placed in safe deposit boxes here. Some other people were on the boxes. And ultimately, the money was taken out to California. Alright, there is knowledge of the fact that he did start with a million seven. Several people know this. Now since 1969, he has spent a good deal of this money and accounting for it is going to be very difficult for Herb [Kalmbach]. For example, he has spent close to $500,000 on private polling. That opens up a whole new thing. It is not illegal, but more of the same thing.

P: Everybody does polling.

D: That's right. There is nothing criminal about it. It's private polling. . . . I don't know of anything that Herb has done that is illegal. . . . What really bothers me is this growing situation. As I say, it is growing because of the continued need to provide support for the Watergate people who are going to hold us up for everything we've got, and the need for some people to perjure themselves as they go down the road here. If this thing ever blows, then we are in a cover up situation. I think it would be extremely damaging to you and the—

P: Sure. The whole concept of Administration justice. Which we cannot have!. . .

D: That's right. I am coming down to what I really think, is that Bob and John and John Mitchell and I can sit down and spend a day, or however long, to figure out one, how this can be carved away from you, so that it does not damage you or the Presidency. It just can't! You are not involved in it and it is something you shouldn't—

P: That is true!. . .

D: What really troubles me is one, will this thing not break some day and the whole thing—domino situation—everything starts crumbling, fingers will be pointing. Bob will be accused of things he has never heard of and deny and try to disprove it. It will get real nasty and just be a real bad situation. And the person who will be hurt by it most will be you and the Presidency, and I just don't think—

P: First, because I am an executive I am supposed to check these things.

D: That's right.

P: Let's come back to this problem. What are your feelings yourself, John? You know what they are all saying. What are your feelings about the chances?

D: I am not confident that we can ride through this. I think there are soft spots. . . .

P: . . . But just looking at it from a cold legal standpoint: you are a lawyer, you were a counsel—doing what you did as counsel. You were not—What would you go to jail for?

D: The obstruction of justice.

P: The obstruction of justice?

D: That is the only one that bothers me.

P: Well, I don't know. I think that one. I feel it could be cut off at the pass, maybe, the obstruction of justice. . . . Talking about your obstruction of justice, though, I don't see it.

D: Well, I have been a conduit for information on taking care of people out there who are guilty of crimes.

P: Oh, you mean like the blackmailers?

D: The blackmailers. Right.

P: Well, I wonder if that part of it can't be—I wonder if that doesn't—let me put it frankly: I wonder if that doesn't have to be continued? Let me put it this way: let us suppose that you get the million bucks, and you get the proper way to handle it. You could hold that side?

D: Uh, huh.

P: It would seem to me that would be worthwhile. . . .

D: There are two routes. One is to figure out how to cut the losses and minimize the human impact and get you up and out and away from it in any way. In a way it would never come back to haunt you. That is one general alternative. The other is to go down the road, just hunker down, fight it at every corner, every turn, don't let people testify—cover it up is what we really are talking about. Just keep it buried, and just hope that we can do it, hope that we make good decisions at the right time, keep our heads cool, we make the right moves.

P: And just take the heat?

D: And just take the heat. . . .

[H. R. Haldeman joins the meeting.]

P: . . . You see, John is concerned, as you know, about the Ehrlichman situation. It worries him a great deal because, and this is why the Hunt problem is so serious, because it had nothing to do with the campaign. It has to do with the Ellsberg case. I don't know what the hell the— (unintelligible)

H[aldeman]: But what I was going to say—

P: What is the answer on this? How you keep it out, I don't know. You can't keep it out if Hunt talks. You see the point is irrelevant. It has gotten to this point—

D: You might put it on a national security basis.

H: It absolutely was.

D: And say that this was—

H: (unintelligible)— CIA—

D: Ah—

H: Seriously.

P: National Security. We had to get information [from Ellsberg's psychiatrist's office] for national security grounds.

D: Then the question is, why didn't the CIA do it or why didn't the FBI do it?

P: Because we had to do it on a confidential basis.

H: Because we were checking them.

P: Neither could be trusted.

H: It has basically never been proven. There was reason to question their position.

P: With the bombing thing coming out and everything coming out, the whole thing was national security.

D: I think we could get by on that.

P: On that one I think we should simply say this was a national security investigation that was conducted. And on that basis, I think . . . Krogh could say he feels he did not perjure himself. He could say it was a national security matter. That is why—. . . You really only have two ways to go. You either decide that the whole (expletive deleted) thing is so full of problems with potential criminal liabilities, which most concern me. I don't give a damn about the publicity. We could rock that through that if we had to let the whole damn thing hang out, and it would be a lousy story for a month. But I can take it. The point is, that I don't want any criminal liabilities. That is the thing that I am concerned about for members of the White House staff, and I would trust for members of the Committee. . . .

H: Well, the thing we talked about yesterday. You have a question where you cut off on this. There is a possibility of cutting it at Liddy, where you are now.

P: Yeah.

D: But to accomplish that requires a continued perjury by Magruder and requires—

P: And requires total commitment and control over all of the defendants which—in other words when they are let down—. . . Another way to do it then Bob, and John realizes this, is to continue to try to cut our losses. Now we have to take a look at that course of action. First it is going to require approximately a million dollars to take care of the jackasses who are in jail. That can be arranged. That could be arranged. But you realize that after we are gone, and assuming we can expend this money, then they are going to crack and it would be an unseemly story. Frankly, all the people aren't going to care that much.

D: That's right.

P: People won't care, but people are going to be talking about it, there is no question. . . . And my point is that I think it is good, frankly, to consider these various options. And then, once you decide on the right plan, you say, "John," you say, "No doubts about the right plan before the election. You handled it just right. You contained it. And now after the election we have to have another plan. Because we can't for four years have this thing eating away." We can't do it.

H: We should change that a little bit. John's point is exactly right. The erosion here now is going to you, and that is the thing that we have to turn off at whatever cost. We have to turn it off at the lowest cost we can, but at whatever cost it takes.

D: That's what we have to do.

P: Well, the erosion is inevitably going to come here, apart from anything and all the people saying well the Watergate isn't a major issue. It isn't. But it will be. It's bound to. (Unintelligible) has to go out. Delaying is the great danger to the White House area. We don't, I say that the White House can't do it. Right?

D: Yes, Sir.

3 Excerpt from the Supreme Court Ruling in the Case of *Roe v. Wade*, 1973

We forthwith acknowledge our awareness of the sensitive and emotional nature of the abortion controversy, of the vigorous opposing views, even among physicians, and of the deep and seemingly absolute convictions that the subject inspires. One's philosophy, one's experiences, one's exposure to the raw edges of human existence, one's religious training, one's attitudes toward life and family and their values, and the moral standards one establishes and seeks to observe, are all likely to influence and to color one's thinking and conclusions about abortion.

In addition, population growth, pollution, poverty, and racial overtones tend to complicate and not to simplify the problem.

Our task, of course, is to resolve the issue by constitutional measurement free of emotion and of predilection. We seek earnestly to do this, and, because we do, we have inquired into, and in this opinion place some emphasis upon, medical and medical-legal history and what that history reveals about man's attitudes toward the abortive procedure over the centuries. . . .

Jane Roe, a single woman who was residing in Dallas County, Texas, instituted this federal action in March 1970 against the District Attorney of the county. She sought a declaratory judgment that the Texas criminal abortion statutes were unconstitutional on their face, and an injunction restraining the defendant from enforcing the statutes.

Roe alleged that she was unmarried and pregnant; that she wished to terminate her pregnancy by an abortion "performed by a competent, licensed physician, under safe, clinical conditions"; that she was unable to get a "legal" abortion in Texas because her life did not appear to be threatened by the continuation of her pregnancy; and that she could not afford to travel to another jurisdiction in order to secure a legal abortion under safe conditions. She claimed that the Texas statutes were unconstitutionally vague and that they abridged her right of personal privacy, protected by the First, Fourth, Fifth, Ninth, and Fourteenth Amendments. By an amendment to her complaint Roe purported to sue "on behalf of herself and all other women" similarly situated. . . .

On the merits, the District Court held that the "fundamental right of single women and married persons to choose whether to have children is protected by the Ninth Amendment, through the Fourteenth Amendment," and that the Texas criminal abortion statutes were void on their face because they were both unconstitutionally vague and constituted an overbroad infringement of the plaintiffs' Ninth Amendment rights. . . .

It perhaps is not generally appreciated that the restrictive criminal abortion laws in effect in a majority of States today are of relatively recent vintage. Those laws, generally proscribing abortion or its attempt at any time during pregnancy except when necessary to preserve the pregnant woman's life, are not of ancient or even of common law origin. Instead, they derive from statutory changes effected, for the most part, in the latter half of the 19th century. . . .

Three reasons have been advanced to explain historically the enactment of criminal abortion laws in the 19th century and to justify their continued existence. . . .

It has been argued occasionally that these laws were the product of a Victorian social concern to discourage illicit sexual conduct. Texas, however, does not advance this justification in the present case, and it appears that no court or commentator has taken the argument seriously. . . .

A second reason is concerned with abortion as a medical procedure. When most criminal abortion laws were first enacted, the procedure was a hazardous one for the woman. This was particularly true prior to the development of antisepsis. . . . Abortion mortality was high. . . . Thus it has been argued that a State's real concern in enacting a criminal abortion law was to protect the pregnant woman, that is, to restrain her from submitting to a procedure that placed her life in serious jeopardy. . . .

The third reason is the State's interest—some phrase it in terms of duty—in protecting prenatal life. . . .

. . . [A]s long as at least *potential* life is involved, the State may assert interests beyond the protection of the pregnant woman alone. . . .

It is with these interests, and the weight to be attached to them, that this case is concerned.

The Constitution does not explicitly mention any right of privacy. In a line of decisions, however, going back perhaps as far as . . . [1891], the Court has recognized that a right of personal privacy, or a guarantee of certain areas or zones of privacy, does exist under the Constitution. . . .

This right of privacy, whether it be founded in the Fourteenth Amendment's concept of personal liberty and restrictions upon state action, as we feel it is, or, as the District Court determined, in the Ninth Amendment's reservation of rights to the people, is broad enough to encompass a woman's decision whether or not to terminate her pregnancy. The detriment that the State would impose upon the pregnant woman by denying this choice altogether is apparent. Specific and direct harm medically diagnosable even in early pregnancy may be involved. Maternity, or additional offspring, may force upon the woman a distressful life and future. Psychological harm may be imminent. Mental and physical health may be taxed by child care. There is also the distress, for all concerned, associated with the unwanted child, and there is the problem of bringing a child into a family already unable, psychologically and otherwise, to care for it. In other cases, as in this one, the additional difficulties and continuing stigma of unwed motherhood may be involved. . . .

On the basis of elements such as these, appellants and some *amici* argue that the woman's right is absolute and that she is entitled to terminate her pregnancy at whatever time, in whatever way, and for whatever reason she alone chooses. With this we do not agree. . . . [A] state may properly assert important interests in safeguarding health, in maintaining medical standards, and in protecting potential life. At some point in pregnancy, these respective interests become sufficiently compelling to sustain regulation of the factors that govern the abortion decision. The privacy right involved, therefore, cannot be said to be absolute. . . .

We therefore conclude that the right of personal privacy includes the abortion decision, but that this right is not unqualified and must be considered against important state interests in regulation. . . .

Where certain "fundamental rights" are involved, the Court has held that regulation limiting these rights may be justified only by a "compelling state interest," . . . and that legislative enactments must be narrowly drawn to express only the legitimate state interests at stake. . . .

. . . The appellee and certain *amici* argue that the fetus is a "person" within the language and meaning of the Fourteenth Amendment. . . .

The Constitution does not define "person" in so many words. . . . All this, together with our observation . . . that throughout the major portion of the 19th century prevailing legal abortion practices were far freer than they are today, persuades us that the word "person," as used in the Fourteenth Amendment, does not include the unborn. . . .

Texas urges that, apart from the Fourteenth Amendment, life begins at conception and is present throughout pregnancy, and that, therefore, the State has a compelling interest in protecting that life from and after conception. We need not resolve the difficult question of when life begins. When those trained in the respective disciplines of medicine, philosophy, and theology are unable to arrive at any consensus, the judiciary, at this point in the development of man's knowledge, is not in a position to speculate as to the answer.

It should be sufficient to note briefly the wide divergence of thinking on this most sensitive and difficult question. . . .

In areas other than criminal abortion the law has been reluctant to endorse any theory that life, as we recognize it, begins before live birth or to accord legal rights to the unborn except in narrowly defined situations and except when the rights are contingent upon live birth. . . . [T]he unborn have never been recognized in the law as persons in the whole sense.

. . . [T]he State does have an important and legitimate interest in preserving and protecting the health of the pregnant woman, whether she be a resident of the State or a nonresident who seeks medical consultation and treatment there, and that it has still another important and legitimate interest in protecting the potentiality of human life. These interests are separate and distinct. Each grows in substantiality as the woman approaches term and, at a point during pregnancy, each becomes "compelling."

With respect to the State's important and legitimate interest in the health of the mother, the "compelling" point, in the light of present medical knowledge, is at approximately the end of the first trimester. This is so because of the now established medical fact, referred to above, that until the end of the first trimester mortality in abortion is less than mortality in normal childbirth. It follows that, from and after this point, a State may regulate the abortion procedure to the extent that the regulation reasonably relates to the preservation and protection of maternal health. . . .

With respect to the State's important and legitimate interest in potential life, the "compelling" point is at viability. This is so because the fetus then presumably has the capability of meaningful life outside the mother's womb. State regulation protective of fetal life after viability thus has both logical and biological justifications. If the State is interested in protecting fetal life after viability, it may go so far as to proscribe abortion during that period except when it is necessary to preserve the life or health of the mother. . . .

To summarize and to repeat:

1. A state criminal abortion statute of the current Texas type, that excepts from criminality only a *life saving* procedure on behalf of the mother, without regard to pregnancy stage and without recognition of the other interests involved, is violative of the Due Process Clause of the Fourteenth Amendment.

(a) For the stage prior to approximately the end of the first trimester, the abortion decision and its effectuation must be left to the medical judgment of the pregnant woman's attending physician.

(b) For the stage subsequent to approximately the end of the first trimester, the State, in promoting its interest in the health of the mother, may, if it chooses, regulate the abortion procedure in ways that are reasonably related to maternal health.

(c) For the stage subsequent to viability the State, in promoting its interest in the potentiality of human life, may, if it chooses, regulate, and even proscribe, abortion except where it is necessary, in appropriate medical judgment, for the preservation of the life or health of the mother. . . .

The decision leaves the State free to place increasing restrictions on abortion as the period of pregnancy lengthens, so long as those restrictions are tailored to the recognized state interests. The decision vindicates the right of the physician to administer medical treatment according to his professional judgment up to the points where important state interests provide compelling justifications for intervention. Up to those points the abortion decision in all its aspects is inherently, and primarily, a medical decision, and basic responsibility for it must rest with the physician. If an individual practitioner abuses the privilege of exercising proper medical judgment, the usual remedies, judicial and intraprofessional, are available.

It is so ordered.

4 "Foresight — and Hindsight": Excerpt from Chapter 11 of the 9/11 Commission Report, 2003

11.3 CAPABILITIES

Earlier chapters describe in detail the actions decided on by the Clinton and Bush administrations. Each president considered or authorized covert actions, a process that consumed considerable time—especially in the Clinton administration—and achieved little success beyond the collection of intelligence. After the August 1998 missile strikes in Afghanistan, naval vessels remained on station in or near the region, prepared to fire cruise missiles. General Hugh Shelton developed as many as 13 different strike options, and did not recommend any of them. The most extended debate on counterterrorism in the Bush administration before 9/11 had to do with missions for the unmanned Predator—whether to use it just to locate Bin Ladin or to wait until it was armed with a missile, so that it could find him and also attack him. Looking back, we are struck with the narrow and unimaginative menu of options for action offered to both President Clinton and President Bush.

Before 9/11, the United States tried to solve the al Qaeda problem with the same government institutions and capabilities it had used in the last stages of the Cold War and its immediate aftermath. These capabilities were insufficient, but little was done to expand or reform them.

For covert action, of course, the White House depended on the Counterterrorist Center and the CIA's Directorate of Operations. Though some officers, particularly in the Bin Ladin unit, were eager for the mission, most were not. The higher management of the directorate was unenthusiastic. The CIA's capacity to conduct paramilitary operations with its own personnel was not large, and the Agency did not seek a large-scale general expansion of these capabilities before 9/11. James Pavitt, the head of this directorate, remembered that covert action, promoted by the White House, had gotten the Clandestine Service into trouble in the past. He had no desire to see this happen again. He thought, not unreasonably, that a truly serious counterterrorism campaign against an enemy of this magnitude would be business primarily for the military, not the Clandestine Service.

As for the Department of Defense, some officers in the Joint Staff were keen to help. Some in the Special Operations Command have told us that they worked on plans for using Special Operations Forces in Afghanistan and that they hoped for action orders. JCS Chairman General Shelton and General Anthony Zinni at Central Command had a different view. Shelton felt that the August 1998 attacks had proved a waste of good ordnance and thereafter consistently opposed firing expensive Tomahawk missiles merely at "jungle gym" terrorist training infrastructure. In this view, he had complete support from Defense Secretary William Cohen. Shelton was prepared to plan other options, but he was also prepared to make perfectly clear his own strong doubts about the wisdom of any military action that risked U.S. lives unless the intelligence was "actionable."

The high price of keeping counterterrorism policy within the restricted circle of the Counterterrorism Security Group and the highest-level principals was nowhere more apparent than in the military establishment. After the August 1998 missile strike, other members of the JCS let the press know their unhappiness that, in conformity with the Goldwater-Nichols reforms, Shelton had been the only member of the JCS to be consulted. Although follow-on military options were briefed more widely, the vice director of operations on the Joint Staff commented to us that intelligence and planning documents relating to al Qaeda arrived in a ziplock red package and that many flag and general officers never had the clearances to see its contents.

At no point before 9/11 was the Department of Defense fully engaged in the mission of countering al Qaeda, though this was perhaps the most dangerous foreign enemy then threatening the United States. The Clinton administration effectively relied on the CIA to take the lead in preparing long-term offensive plans against an enemy sanctuary. The Bush administration adopted this approach, although its emerging new strategy envisioned some yet undefined further role for the military in addressing the problem. Within Defense, both Secretary Cohen and Secretary Donald Rumsfeld gave their principal attention to other challenges.

America's homeland defenders faced outward. NORAD itself was barely able to retain any alert bases. Its planning scenarios occasionally considered the danger of hijacked aircraft being guided to American targets, but only aircraft that were coming from overseas. We recognize that a costly change in NORAD's defense posture to deal with the danger of suicide hijackers, before such a threat had ever actually been realized, would have been a tough sell. But NORAD did not canvass available intelligence and try to make the case.

The most serious weaknesses in agency capabilities were in the domestic arena. In chapter 3 we discussed these institutions—the FBI, the Immigration and Naturalization Service, the FAA, and others. The major pre-9/11 effort to strengthen domestic agency capabilities came in 2000, as part of a millennium after-action review. President Clinton and his principal advisers paid considerable attention then to border security problems, but were not able to bring about significant improvements before leaving office. The NSC-led interagency process did not effectively bring along the leadership of the Justice and Transportation departments in an agenda for institutional change.

The FBI did not have the capability to link the collective knowledge of agents in the field to national priorities. The acting director of the FBI did not learn of his Bureau's hunt for two possible al Qaeda operatives in the United States or about his Bureau's arrest of an Islamic extremist taking flight training until September 11. The director of central intelligence knew about the FBI's Moussaoui investigation weeks before word of it made its way even to the FBI's own assistant director for counterterrorism.

Other agencies deferred to the FBI. In the August 6 PDB reporting to President Bush of 70 full-field investigations related to al Qaeda, news the President said he found heartening, the CIA had simply restated what the FBI had said. No one looked behind the curtain.

The FAA's capabilities to take aggressive, anticipatory security measures were especially weak. Any serious policy examination of a suicide hijacking scenario, critiquing each of the layers of the security system, could have suggested changes to fix glaring vulnerabilities—expanding no-fly lists, searching passengers identified by the CAPPS screening system, deploying Federal Air Marshals domestically, hardening cockpit doors, alerting air crew to a different kind of hijacking than what they had been trained to expect, or adjusting the training of controllers and managers in the FAA and NORAD.

Government agencies also sometimes display a tendency to match capabilities to mission by defining away the hardest part of their job. They are often passive, accepting what are viewed as givens, including that efforts to identify and fix glaring vulnerabilities to dangerous threats would be too costly, too controversial, or too disruptive.

11.4 MANAGEMENT

Operational Management

Earlier in this report we detailed various missed opportunities to thwart the 9/11 plot. Information was not shared, sometimes inadvertently or because of legal misunderstandings. Analysis was not pooled. Effective operations were not launched. Often the handoffs of information were lost across the divide separating the foreign and domestic agencies of the government.

However the specific problems are labeled, we believe they are symptoms of the government's broader inability to adapt how it manages problems to the new challenges of the twenty-first century. The agencies are like a set of specialists in a hospital, each ordering tests, looking for symptoms, and prescribing medications. What is missing is the attending physician who makes sure they work as a team.

One missing element was effective management of transnational operations. Action officers should have drawn on all available knowledge in the government. This management should have ensured that information was shared and duties were clearly assigned across agencies, and across the foreign-domestic divide.

Consider, for example, the case of Mihdhar, Hazmi, and their January 2000 trip to Kuala Lumpur, detailed in chapter 6. In late 1999, the National Security Agency (NSA) analyzed communications associated with a man named Khalid, a man named Nawaf, and a man named Salem. Working-level officials in the intelligence community knew little more than this. But they correctly concluded that "Nawaf" and "Khalid" might be part of "an operational cadre" and that "something nefarious might be afoot."

The NSA did not think its job was to research these identities. It saw itself as an agency to support intelligence consumers, such as CIA. The NSA tried to respond energetically to any request made. But it waited to be asked.

If NSA had been asked to try to identify these people, the agency would have started by checking its own database of earlier information from these same sources. Some of this information had been reported; some had not. But it was all readily accessible in the database. NSA's analysts would promptly have discovered who Nawaf was, that his full name might be Nawaf al Hazmi, and that he was an old friend of Khalid.

With this information and more that was available, managers could have more effectively tracked the movement of these operatives in southeast Asia. With the name "Nawaf al Hazmi," a manager could then have asked the State Department also to check that name. State would promptly have found its own record on Nawaf al Hazmi, showing that he too had been issued a visa to visit the United States. Officials would have learned that the visa had been issued at the same place—Jeddah—and on almost the same day as the one given to Khalid al Mihdhar.

When the travelers left Kuala Lumpur for Bangkok, local officials were able to identify one of the travelers as Khalid al Mihdhar. After the flight left, they learned that one of his companions had the name Alhazmi. But the officials did not know what that name meant.

The information arrived at Bangkok too late to track these travelers as they came in. Had the authorities there already been keeping an eye out for Khalid al Mihdhar as part of a general regional or worldwide alert, they might have tracked him coming in. Had they been alerted to look for a possible companion named Nawaf al Hazmi, they might have noticed him too. Instead, they were notified only after Kuala Lumpur sounded the alarm. By that time, the travelers had already disappeared into the streets of Bangkok.

On January 12, the head of the CIA's al Qaeda unit told his bosses that surveillance in Kuala Lumpur was continuing. He may not have known that in fact Mihdhar and his companions had dispersed and the tracking was falling apart. U.S. officials in Bangkok regretfully reported the bad news on January 13. The names they had were put on a watchlist in Bangkok, so that Thai authorities might notice if the men left the country. On January 14, the head of the CIA's al Qaeda unit again updated his bosses, telling them that officials were continuing to track the suspicious individuals who had now dispersed to various countries.

Unfortunately, there is no evidence of any tracking efforts actually being undertaken by anyone after the Arabs disappeared into Bangkok. No other effort was made to create other opportunities to spot these Arab travelers in case the screen in Bangkok failed. Just from the evidence in Mihdhar's passport, one of the logical possible destinations and interdiction points would have been the United States. Yet no one alerted the INS or the FBI to look for these individuals. They arrived, unnoticed, in Los Angeles on January 15.

In early March 2000, Bangkok reported that Nawaf al Hazmi, now identified for the first time with his full name, had departed on January 15 on a United Airlines flight to Los Angeles. Since the CIA did not appreciate the significance of that name or notice the cable, we have found no evidence that this information was sent to the FBI.

Even if watchlisting had prevented or at least alerted U.S. officials to the entry of Hazmi and Mihdhar, we do not think it is likely that watchlisting, by itself, have prevented the 9/11 attacks. Al Qaeda adapted to the failure of some of its operatives to gain entry into the United States. None of these future hijackers was a pilot. Alternatively, had they been permitted entry and surveilled, some larger results might have been possible had the FBI been patient.

These are difficult what-ifs. The intelligence community might have judged that the risks of conducting such a prolonged intelligence operation were too high—potential terrorists might have been lost track of, for example. The pre-9/11 FBI might not have been judged capable of conducting such an operation. But surely the intelligence community would have preferred to have the chance to make these choices.

From the details of this case, or from the other opportunities we catalogue in the text box [see the ten Operational Opportunities listed below], one can see how hard it is for the intelligence community to assemble enough of the puzzle pieces gathered by different agencies to make some sense of them and then develop a fully informed joint plan. Accomplishing all this is especially difficult in a transnational case. We sympathize with the working-level officers, drowning in information and trying to decide what is important or what needs to be done when no particular action has been requested of them.

Who had the job of managing the case to make sure these things were done? One answer is that everyone had the job. The CIA's deputy director for operations, James Pavitt, stressed to us that the responsibility resided with all involved. Above all he emphasized the primacy of the field. The field had the lead in managing operations. The job of headquarters, he stressed, was to support the field, and do so without delay. If the field asked for information or other support, the job of headquarters was to get it—right away.

This is a traditional perspective on operations and, traditionally, it has had great merit. It reminded us of the FBI's pre-9/11 emphasis on the primacy of its field offices. When asked about how this traditional structure would adapt to the challenge of managing a transnational case, one that hopped from place to place as this one did, the deputy director argued that all involved were responsible for making it work. Pavitt underscored the responsibility of the particular field location where the suspects were being tracked at any given time. On the other hand, he also said that the Counterterrorist Center was supposed to manage all the moving parts, while what happened on the ground was the responsibility of managers in the field.

Headquarters tended to support and facilitate, trying to make sure everyone was in the loop. From time to time a particular post would push one way, or headquarters would urge someone to do something. But headquarters never really took responsibility for the successful management of this case. Hence the managers at CIA headquarters did not realize that omissions in planning had occurred, and they scarcely knew that the case had fallen apart.

The director of the Counterterrorist Center at the time, Cofer Black, recalled to us that this operation was one among many and that, at the time, it was "considered interesting, but not heavy water yet." He recalled the failure to get the word to Bangkok fast enough, but has no evident recollection of why the case then dissolved, unnoticed.

The next level down, the director of the al Qaeda unit in CIA at the time recalled that he did not think it was his job to direct what should or should not be done. He did not pay attention when the individuals dispersed and things fell apart. There was no conscious decision to stop the operation after the trail was temporarily lost in Bangkok. He acknowledged, however, that perhaps there had been a letdown for his overworked staff after the extreme tension and long hours in the period of the millennium alert.

The details of this case illuminate real management challenges, past and future. The U.S. government must find a way of pooling intelligence and using it to guide the planning of and assignment of responsibilities for *joint operations* involving organizations as disparate as the CIA, the FBI, the State Department, the military, and the agencies involved in homeland security.

Operational Opportunities

1. January 2000: the CIA does not watchlist Khalid al Mihdhar or notify the FBI when it learned Mihdhar possessed a valid U.S. visa.
2. January 2000: the CIA does not develop a transnational plan for tracking Mihdhar and his associates so that they could be followed to Bangkok and onward, including the United States.
3. March 2000: the CIA does not watchlist Nawaf al Hazmi or notify the FBI when it learned that he possessed a U.S. visa and had flown to Los Angeles on January 15, 2000.
4. January 2001: the CIA does not inform the FBI that a source had identified Khallad, or Tawfiq bin Attash, a major figure in the October 2000 bombing of the USS *Cole*, as having attended the meeting in Kuala Lumpur with Khalid al Mihdhar.
5. May 2001: a CIA official does not notify the FBI about Mihdhar's U.S. visa, Hazmi's U.S. travel, or Khallad's having attended the Kuala Lumpur meeting (identified when he reviewed all of the relevant traffic because of the high level of threats).
6. June 2001: FBI and CIA officials do not ensure that all relevant information regarding the Kuala Lumpur meeting was shared with the *Cole* investigators at the June 11 meeting.

7. August 2001: the FBI does not recognize the significance of the information regarding Mihdhar and Hazmi's possible arrival in the United States and thus does not take adequate action to share information, assign resources, and give sufficient priority to the search.
8. August 2001: FBI headquarters does not recognize the significance of the information regarding Moussaoui's training and beliefs and thus does not take adequate action to share information, involve higher-level officials across agencies, obtain information regarding Moussaoui's ties to al Qaeda, and give sufficient priority to determining what Moussaoui might be planning.
9. August 2001: the CIA does not focus on information that Khalid Sheikh Mohammed is a key al Qaeda lieutenant or connect information identifying KSM as the "Mukhtar" mentioned in other reports to the analysis that could have linked "Mukhtar" with Ramzi Binalshibh and Moussaoui.
10. August 2001: the CIA and FBI do not connect the presence of Mihdhar, Hazmi, and Moussaoui to the general threat reporting about imminent attacks.

Institutional Management

Beyond those day-to-day tasks of bridging the foreign-domestic divide and matching intelligence with plans, the challenges include broader management issues pertaining to how the top leaders of the government set priorities and allocate resources. Once again it is useful to illustrate the problem by examining the CIA, since before 9/11 this agency's role was so central in the government's counterterrorism efforts.

On December 4, 1998, DCI Tenet issued a directive to several CIA officials and his deputy for community management, stating: "We are at war. I want no resources or people spared in this effort, either inside CIA or the Community." The memorandum had little overall effect on mobilizing the CIA or the intelligence community.

The memo was addressed only to CIA officials and the deputy for community management, Joan Dempsey. She faxed the memo to the heads of the major intelligence agencies after removing covert action sections. Only a handful of people received it. The NSA director at the time, Lieutenant General Kenneth Minihan, believed the memo applied only to the CIA and not the NSA, because no one had informed him of any NSA shortcomings. For their part, CIA officials thought the memorandum was intended for the rest of the intelligence community, given that they were already doing all they could and believed that the rest of the community needed to pull its weight.

The episode indicates some of the limitations of the DCI's authority over the direction and priorities of the intelligence community, especially its elements within the Department of Defense. The DCI has to direct agencies without controlling them. He does not receive an appropriation for their activities, and therefore does not control their purse strings. He has little insight into how they spend their resources. Congress attempted to strengthen the DCI's authority in 1996 by creating the positions of deputy DCI for community management and assistant DCIs for collection, analysis and production, and administration. But the authority of these positions is limited, and the vision of central management clearly has not been realized.